الاستنباط من البحر العميق

AL- ISTINBĀTU MIN AL BAHRI AL A'MÌQ

DROPS FROM THE DEEP OCEAN

REFLECTIONS ON THE QUR'AN

Cycles of Difficulty and Ease

with a focus on

► Contemporary Renderings
► Psychological Explorations
► Western Discourses
► Lexical Analysis

VOLUME 9

Dr. M. Yunus Kumek

Address to the Islamic Religious Scholars & Philosophers

Cover Photo by Y. Kumek, Alexandria, Egypt, January 12, 2019.

Medina House
publishing

www.medinahouse.org
170 Manhattan Ave, Po. Box 63
New York 14215
contact@medinahouse.org

Published in the United States of America.

TABLE OF CONTENTS

VOLUME 9

VOLUME 9

Sûrah 2 – al-Baqara

[25]

وَبَشِّرِ الَّذِينَ آمَنُواْ وَعَمِلُواْ الصَّالِحَاتِ أَنَّ لَهُمْ جَنَّاتٍ تَجْرِي مِن تَحْتِهَا الأَنْهَارُ كُلَّمَا رُزِقُواْ مِنْهَا مِن ثَمَرَةٍ رِّزْقاً قَالُواْ هَذَا الَّذِي رُزِقْنَا مِن قَبْلُ وَأُتُواْ بِهِ مُتَشَابِهاً وَلَهُمْ فِيهَا أَزْوَاجٌ مُّطَهَّرَةٌ وَهُمْ فِيهَا خَالِدُونَ {25/البقرة}[1]

Need for Motivation: A Human Reality

One should remember that as humans we need constant encouragement and motivation in life to continue to struggle on the path of Allah ﷻ. One can review the ayahs of the Qurān with a similar meaning of بَشِّرِ.

As humans we tend to do get tired, unmotivated, and discouraged due to our impatience as mentioned[2] {155/البقرة} وَبَشِّرِ الصَّابِرِينَ. We try to struggle for the sake of Allah ﷻ and yet, get broken hearted and hopeless due to not seeing the products of our efforts.

This can be in the engagements of children in their upbringing or in student-teacher relationships. It is very difficult to be patient when a parent is interacting with his or her child showing constantly attitude, and disrespect. It is very difficult to be patient treating them kindly and patiently expecting the good results later while being treated rudely at the moment. Even if the person realizes the good outcome of the times when the person was patient, yet it is very difficult constantly remind oneself the requirement of patience.

One should remember that imān is the source of real motivation and encouragement as mentioned[3] {223/البقرة} وَبَشِّرِ الْمُؤْمِنِينَ and وَبَشِّرِ الَّذِينَ آمَنُواْ. A person who has imān to Allah ﷻ expects things from Allah

---

1. And give good tidings to those who believe and do righteous deeds that they will have gardens [in Paradise] beneath which rivers flow. Whenever they are provided with a provision of fruit therefrom, they will say, "This is what we were provided with before." And it is given to them in likeness. And they will have therein purified spouses, and they will abide therein eternally.
2. And We will surely test you with something of fear and hunger and a loss of wealth and lives and fruits, but give good tidings to the patient,
3. Your wives are a place of sowing of seed for you, so come to your place of cultivation however you wish and put forth [righteousness] for yourselves. And fear Allah and know that you will meet Him. And give

☙ that a person who does not have imān, does not have any of these expectations. This is mentioned as[4] وَلاَ تَهِنُواْ فِي ابْتِغَاءِ الْقَوْمِ إِن تَكُونُواْ تَأْلَمُونَ فَإِنَّهُمْ يَأْلَمُونَ كَمَا تَأْلَمونَ وَتَرْجُونَ مِنَ اللهِ مَا لاَ يَرْجُونَ وَكَانَ اللهُ عَلِيمًا حَكِيمًا {النساء/104}. Therefore, motivating oneself with imān to please Allah ☙ gives the person hope, encouragement and expectation of the good results from only Allah ☙.

Yet, we forget this reality. We want to see the gains on our investments of struggle on the path of Allah ☙ in this life immediately. Yet, a person of imān in reality does not expect anything even a result in this life. He or she expects everything from Allah ☙ regardless of the results of this achievement either being a failure or an achievement in this life.

Yet, we are human beings. The realities of بَشَرٍ can indicate that we can't sometimes reach the levels of ideal state of motivation for the sake of Allah ☙ at the times of absence of results of our efforts. We get so hopeless, disappointed, demotivated and lose our sleeps. Allah ☙ motivates us in the Qurān with these reminders.

In this regard, the ayah[5] أَكَانَ لِلنَّاسِ عَجَبًا أَنْ أَوْحَيْنَا إِلَى رَجُلٍ مِّنْهُمْ أَنْ أَنذِرِ النَّاسَ وَبَشِّرِ الَّذِينَ آمَنُواْ أَنَّ لَهُمْ قَدَمَ صِدْقٍ عِندَ رَبِّهِمْ قَالَ الْكَافِرُونَ إِنَّ هَذَا لَسَاحِرٌ مُبِينٌ {يونس/2} can be very interesting and critical to analyze when we focus on the expression وَبَشِّرِ الَّذِينَ آمَنُواْ أَنَّ لَهُمْ قَدَمَ صِدْقٍ عِندَ رَبِّهِمْ.

In our engagements of struggle on the path of Allah ☙, sometimes expecting results of our struggles can be in reality related to expectation of recognition for our engagements. Yet, in their reality, all the recognitions, approvals and results are in vain unless they have a recognition, approval and a position with Allah ☙. Even the cases of sadaqa-i jariya as encouraged by Rasulullah ﷺ can motivate the person to engage in long-lasting amal after one dies. Yes, we need to struggle for this as ordered by Rasulullah ﷺ. Yet, all amal have value and real position with Allah ☙.

In this regard, Allah ☙ mentions that a believer who follows the path of Rasulullah ﷺ with sunnah can inshAllah have an honorable position

---

4. And do not weaken in pursuit of the enemy. If you should be suffering - so are they suffering as you are suffering, but you expect from Allah that which they expect not. And Allah is ever Knowing and Wise.

5. And give to the orphans their properties and do not substitute the defective [of your own] for the good [of theirs]. And do not consume their properties into your own. Indeed, that is ever a great sin.

with Allah ﷻ regardless of the results of their amal as mentioned[6] أَكَانَ لِلنَّاسِ عَجَبًا أَنْ أَوْحَيْنَا إِلَى رَجُلٍ مِّنْهُمْ أَنْ أَنذِرِ النَّاسَ وَبَشِّرِ الَّذِينَ آمَنُواْ أَنَّ لَهُمْ قَدَمَ صِدْقٍ عِندَ رَبِّهِمْ قَالَ الْكَافِرُونَ إِنَّ هَذَا لَسَاحِرٌ مُّبِينٌ {يونس/2}.

وَبَشِّرِ and[8] وَبَشِّرِ الْمُخْبِتِينَ {الحج/34} One can also review the ayahs with[7] الْمُحْسِنِينَ {الحج/37} that Allah ﷻ mentions an encouraging glad tiding that have the qualities of ikhlas, humbleness, taslim, and ihsan. These people are the ones who go above and beyond in their engagements for the sake of Allah ﷻ.

One should remember that iman and good action-amalu salih have complementary roles to enter into Jannah with the Fadl and Karam of Allah ﷻ.

[28]

كَيْفَ تَكْفُرُونَ بِاللَّهِ وَكُنتُمْ أَمْوَاتاً فَأَحْيَاكُمْ ثُمَّ يُمِيتُكُمْ ثُمَّ يُحْيِيكُمْ ثُمَّ إِلَيْهِ تُرْجَعُونَ {البقرة/28}[9]

When we analyze this ayah, one can realize the styles of iltifat that Allah ﷻ directly addresses compared to third pronoun style of addressing. When we analyze this style within the context of this ayah, one can realize that there is an emphasis for humans to realize the ni'mahs of Allah ﷻ. In this regard, there is an emphasis especially on the ni'mahs of Allah ﷻ that humans can realize immediately, and clearly that they are dependent on them.

---

6. Have the people been amazed that We revealed [revelation] to a man from among them, [saying], "Warn mankind and give good tidings to those who believe that they will have a [firm] precedence of honor with their Lord"? [But] the disbelievers say, "Indeed, this is an obvious magician."
7. And for all religion We have appointed a rite [of sacrifice] that they may mention the name of Allah over what He has provided for them of [sacrificial] animals. For your god is one God, so to Him submit. And, [O Muhammad], give good tidings to the humble [before their Lord]
8. Their meat will not reach Allah, nor will their blood, but what reaches Him is piety from you. Thus have We subjected them to you that you may glorify Allah for that [to] which He has guided you; and give good tidings to the doers of good.
9. How can you disbelieve in Allah when you were lifeless and He brought you to life; then He will cause you to die, then He will bring you [back] to life, and then to Him you will be returned.

Atoms in Human Body

When we think about the atoms in human body, one can ask a very basic question: where do they come from? How do they act? How do they get together? Why do they get together?

For the sake of discussion, we are not using today's identifiable named smallest particles in particle physics as for example electrons, protons, hadrons, mesons, or quarks and others, since the word atom has become a popular term among humans to identify smallest part in things, therefore we use this term.

Going back to our original discussion, one can find a lot of atoms in the universe. An atom is the basic form of an element. Each element in particle physics have different number electrons, protons and subatomic particles.

In subatomic physics, protons and nucleons are in the nucleus have more stable states than electrons. Due to this stability, in denotations or classifications, element's atomic number is assigned due to their number of protons. The mass of this atom or element is denoted with mass of protons and neutrons where other subatomic particles assumed to have a negligible mass compared to protons and neutrons. Matter is generally defined to be a substance that occupies mass and space [1].

When we consider a human body, it is formed of billions of atoms. Then, there are classifications as these atoms form groups. They can be called in an enlarging scales compounds, amino acids, protein, DNA, nucleus, cell, organism, bacteria, tissue, organ, systems and body.

On the other hand, atoms present in a chair to form them, on a desk, lamp, cat, dog, pen, star, and other matters.

According to current humans scientific understanding, elements or atoms are same in each substance, matter or being. Then, the basic question how does a human body is formed but not a tree? Who decides all the distribution of the basic elements?

The answer is simple and straightforward: Allah ﷻ with Divine Destiny, Qadar, and al-Gayb orders everything "to be" in their assigned

وَهُوَ الْخَلَّاقُ الْعَلِيمُ {يس/81} إِنَّمَا أَمْرُهُ إِذَا أَرَادَ شَيْئًا أَنْ يَقُولَ position as mentioned[10] لَهُ كُنْ فَيَكُونُ {يس/82} فَسُبْحَانَ الَّذِي بِيَدِهِ مَلَكُوتُ كُلِّ شَيْءٍ وَإِلَيْهِ تُرْجَعُونَ {يس/83}

In this above ayah, one can realize that Allah ﷻ can create, form, and decide. Yet, this Divine Decisions in creation, fomations and decisions as can be referred as Qadar or al-Ghayb is only known by Allah ﷻ as mentioned {يس/81} وَهُوَ الْخَلَّاقُ الْعَلِيمُ. There is no human causality systems or methodology or usul in these given initial positions to the substances or matters as mentioned {يس/82} إِنَّمَا أَمْرُهُ إِذَا أَرَادَ شَيْئًا أَنْ يَقُولَ لَهُ كُنْ فَيَكُونُ.

The expression كُنْ فَيَكُونُ can eliminate and remove humans causality system as a primary usûl and can indicate the emphasis of the Divine Mashiyyah of Allah ﷻ as mentioned إِنَّمَا أَمْرُهُ إِذَا أَرَادَ شَيْئًا.

Yet, one should remember that these are especially the parts for humans that they should make constant tasbìh and tanzih with SubhanAllah due to their limited wrong renderings about the Infinite Transcendent Reality of Allah ﷻ in the realms of al-Ghayb, Qadar, -Divine Destiny and embody the notion of humbleness and humility with taslim and tawakkul to the Infinite Ownership, Authority and Dominion of Allah ﷻ as mentioned بِيَدِهِ مَلَكُوتُ كُلِّ شَيْءٍ.

Second, humans cannot understand the life given to the beings with their causalities. In other words, if the same combination of elements come together, humans cannot generate life. Existence of life is a direct intervention of Allah ﷻ without any causalities, scientific means or laws as mentioned[11] إِذْ قَالَ رَبُّكَ لِلْمَلَائِكَةِ إِنِّي خَالِقٌ بَشَرًا مِن طِينٍ {ص/71} فَإِذَا سَوَّيْتُهُ وَنَفَخْتُ فِيهِ مِن رُوحِي فَقَعُوا لَهُ سَاجِدِينَ {ص/72}

In this above ayah, one can realize that Allah ﷻ mentions the matter/substance as طِينٍ in {ص/71} إِنِّي خَالِقٌ بَشَرًا مِن طِينٍ. This can indicate the body and form. The life is given into this body as indicated with the word rûh and directly attributed to Allah ﷻ as mentioned فَإِذَا سَوَّيْتُهُ وَنَفَخْتُ فِيهِ مِن رُوحِي

---

10. Is not He who created the heavens and the earth Able to create the likes of them? Yes, [it is so]; and he is the Knowing Creator. His command is only when He intends a thing that He says to it, "Be," and it is. So exalted is He in whose hand is the realm of all things, and to Him you will be returned.

11. [So mention] when your Lord said to the angels, "Indeed, I am going to create a human being from clay. So when I have proportioned him and breathed into him of My [created] soul, then fall down to him in prostration."

To summarize above points, the primary but essential two questions are:

1. Who Decides where all the elements will be formed in a human body, plant, cat, fish, star? The answer is simple and straightforward that Allah ﷻ decides with the Divine Mashiyyah, Qadar, Yaf'alu ma yashāu with kun-fayakun and al-Gayb

2. Who Gives Life to the substances and elements although humans can bring the same combination of elements but cannot give life? The answer is simple and straightforward that Allah ﷻ gives life without any causalities, reason, human realm.

One can remember rûh is a life as mentioned in the Qurān and Sunnah of Rasulullah ﷺ that humans not know much about it as mentioned وَيَسْأَلُونَكَ عَنِ الرُّوحِ قُلِ الرُّوحُ مِنْ أَمْرِ رَبِّي وَمَا أُوتِيتُم مِّن الْعِلْمِ إِلاَّ قَلِيلاً {الإسراء/85}[12]. Allah ﷻ directly attributed this on the Divine Dhat as[13] فَإِذَا سَوَّيْتُهُ وَنَفَخْتُ فِيهِ مِن رُّوحِي فَقَعُوا لَهُ سَاجِدِينَ {ص/72}

All above simple realities necessitate La ilaha illa Allah. This reality is simple, straightforward, clear, and accessible to everyone.

Unfortunately, one of the traps of Shaytān is that a person lost in the above and detailed steps of means and causalities forget their starting point of purpose, meaning, and goal of being in this mental, intellectual and physical journey.

In the above detailed and complex steps of classifications of atoms forming groups, compounds, amino acids, protein, DNA, nucleus, cell, organism, bacteria, tissue, organ, systems and bodies and complex and perfect systems, humans get amazed with the means but lost in the journey without finding the end, the real and main goal.

It is similar to someone entering an amazing house and being amazed with the door knobs, sofa, floor designs but don't want to know the owner of the house to express his amazement and gratitude. This is the end goal.

Yet, this end and real goal is very simple and accessible to everyone with La ilaha illa Allah.

---

12. And they ask you, [O Muhammad], about the soul. Say, "The soul is of the affair of my Lord. And mankind have not been given of knowledge except a little."
13. So when I have proportioned him and breathed into him of My [created] soul, then fall down to him in prostration."

Sometimes, the arrogance of having some understanding of these complexities through science or philosophy make the person of the scientific intellectual humiliate this simple reality of tawhid. He or she is bothered with the simplicity of availability of this reality to all levels of learners. Then, he or she tries to generate assumed artificial and complex looking renderings through statistical arguments, hypothesis and assumptions.

At the end of the day, he or she deifies a socially constructed terms sucha as nature, science or scientific laws hiding the One, God, Adonai or Allah as the Absolute and Real Reality behind.

One should know that the real goal should be very simple and accessible to everyone. Yet it is the case and it is La ilaha illa Allah.

La ilaha illa Allah is a reality and accessible required sustenance of the existence.

Air is a reality and accessible required sustenance of the existence.

The idea of exclusivity, limiting access of the primary sustenance stems from arrogance.

Therefore, for some of the diseased hearts the reason that they don't want to accept La ilaha illa Allah is that they don't want a reality that is accessible to everyone but they want something only exclusively rendered and deduced by them.

The same diseased hearts don't realize that air is accessible to everyone simply and clearly with the Grace of Allah ﷻ but still it is reality of being primary sustenance for existence.

Similarly, if air is the primary sustenance for existence for the body, then La ilaha illa Allah (imān) is the primary sustenance for existence for the rûh.

Life-Existence

Life is the biggest ni'mah of Allah ﷻ. Life is the most mysterious ni'mah of Allah ﷻ. Life is the highest n'imah of Allah ﷻ above others. Life is the most obvious and clear ni'mah of Allah ﷻ.

Life and existence can transform a miniscule and trivial looking thing into something important and very critical.

One can realize that Allah ﷻ emphasizes in this ayah the importance of existence compared to non-existence.

This is mentioned with the expression وَكُنتُمْ أَمْوَ اتاً فَأَحْيَاكُمْ. It is important to realize the main criteria in our purpose that comes with existence. Life or hayāt in Arabic can indicate this primary ni'mah of Allah ﷻ that we don't realize but we take it as granted.

One of the basics flows of modern philosophy is that they take life and existence as granted or sometimes with possibilities.

For example, Descartes famous quota as ""I think; therefore, I am" all assume life in their furthering of philosophy.

Yet, Allah ﷻ reminds people this basic given primary required n'imah of life. If there is no life, there is no person, ideas, thoughts and anything. William Shakespeare's in the play of Hamlet underlines this reality with his quota of "to be or not to be that is the question."

SubhanAllah! Allah ﷻ is al-Hayy, the Source of All lives and the Absolute, Infinite, Required, and Independent Life. Yet, we receive the reflection of this Name and Attribute of Allah ﷻ in our existence.

Cancer, Malignant Cells & Existence of Allah ﷻ

One should remember that Allah ﷻ gives humans different signs to revisit their interpretations of life, science, incidents, occurrences and nature.

In the increased popularized notions of evolution theory as adapted by all the public schools in non-Muslim countries and even some Muslim countries, one should have been really uncomfortable how a theory can statistically argue a type of absurd-meaning for each cell in its life and existence as a self-randomized automated being and then claim explicitly and implicitly non-existence of God Who is the Real Doer, the Real Cause, and the Real Sustainer of all cells, units of life, and the universe made of different elements?

If this trend was one of the peripheral trends in the world, that would not have been a much deal but a deal or a problem of minority. Yet, this popularized trend affirmed and enforced by the policies as a way and perspective of life. This trend automatically brought forth distancing and alienating people from the Real Doer, the Real Sustainer and the Real Creator of everything, Allah ﷻ.

Every action has a reaction as part of the sunnatullah. This huge impacted forced effect of evolution theory idolized, politicized, and supported life perspective given to the children, youth, students, and adults curriculumized at different levels of formal and informal educational settings have really made the people choose either religion, God as a backwards phenomenon or science, evolution theory as a modern, cool and popular approach.

Regardless of people followed these trends intentionally or unintentionally, or logically or not, when majority of people have justified becoming ungrateful, unappreciative and denial of God in life perspectives, possibly, (Allahu A'lam), then Allah ﷻ has sent a reminder or a phenomenon known and visible by scientific communities.

This phenomenon called cancerous or malignant cells randomly without any seeming purpose or meaning occurred in human bodies and spread through other organs.

Yet, in this deification of era of the verge of 21st century of cells, DNA and claiming statistical arguments of self-existence and life through enforced evolution theory related-life perspectives, the cause of occurrence or initial start of these random or evil-looking cells is still unidentified.

One should remember that life-existence of any being at a level of cell or at a level of human being is one of the biggest and obvious miracles of Allah ﷻ. In this regard, one can really witness clear cover of causalities in the life-existence of any being including cells benign or malignant cells or in the life-existence of humans or universes.

This reality is mentioned as[14] إِنَّمَا أَمْرُهُ إِذَا أَرَادَ شَيْئًا أَنْ يَقُولَ لَهُ كُنْ فَيَكُونُ {يس/82}. The reality of كُنْ فَيَكُونُ is a reminder for us that Allah ﷻ is the Real Doer and causalities are only means of creation.

The cover of casualties, the appearance of unidentified cells malignant or benign is another possible sign for us to remind us the Real Doer of everything beyond causalities, meanings, and scientific methodology of cause and effect.

Miracles as a good-looking incidents or cancer as an evil-looking catastrophe are reminders for us for the breaking points of causalities.

Yet, Allah ﷻ established the life and nature on the bases of causalities as part of the sunnatullah so that the cover with causalities or science is not fully removed on the path of self-struggle to find Allah ﷻ.

---

14. His command is only when He intends a thing that He says to it, "Be," and it is.

Life-Existence the Biggest and the Obvious Miracle of Allah ﷻ

Cover of Causalities

One should really ponder closely upon the ayah إِنَّمَا أَمْرُهُ إِذَا أَرَادَ شَيْئًا أَنْ يَقُولَ لَهُ كُنْ فَيَكُونُ {82/يس} and وَكُنْتُمْ أَمْوَاتاً فَأَحْيَاكُمْ.

In almost all creation of Allah ﷻ, one can see the causalities cover perhaps as a very thin and transparent layer in front of the Direct Intervention of Allah ﷻ.

One can call these causalities as sunnatullah, the laws -both scientific and social laws as established by Allah ﷻ.

Especially, one can realize the layer of causalities a little bit thicker in the engagements of what human consider as evil in order humans not blame Allah ﷻ, astagfiruallah. The deaths due to heart attacks, cancer, accidents, virus and other all others can be a little thicker cover of causalities. As a trial or test, most humans seem to run behind these causalities and implicitly idolize them instead of taking refuge in Allah ﷻ, the Real Cause of All Causalities.

Yet, this thick cover of causalities above undesired and evil-looking incidents are in a sense Rahmah, Fadl and Grace for humans that they don't blame Allah ﷻ immediately without any adab, astagfirullah and lose their most important asset of imān for this life and afterlife.

Life without any Causality

When we ponder on life and existence, there is no causality between existence-life and non-existence as established by Allah ﷻ in وَكُنْتُمْ أَمْوَاتاً فَأَحْيَاكُمْ and كُنْ فَيَكُونُ.

This is the biggest miracle without any causality happening continuously and showing clearly and explicitly Allah ﷻ.

One can ask what is the hikmah of having no-causality for life-existence? Allah ﷻ could have made life through the means of causalities as well.

Life is the purest form of ni'mah without any possible rendering of evil that does not necessitate a cover of causality.

This pure and primary ni'mah is directly without any cover and causality attributed to Allah ﷻ.

Today, the dilemma of all scientists and scientific communities who are not aware of this reality is the notion of sidetracking this reality.

If a person looks into simple biological arguments advocating evolution in the pursuit of distancing people from Allah SWT miss this simple reality for the base of their argument.

Yet, all other arguments then become shaky if the base is not strong.

In arguments of evolution, there are parts of logic that is in line with the realities mentioned in the Qurān. Yet, when there is the mix of truth based on some assumptions and wrong premises, then the argument itself becomes questionable.

If we really consider the arguments of life-existence at subatomic levels and lower levels and forming structures and systems, always the simple question is asked as "who gives them the order to form a structure of an eye, ear, tail, planet, star, fish and all others?" This basic premise is missing. This was explained also in previous sections.

In this regard, Allah ﷻ directly attributes life and existence without any causality to Divine Self with كُنْ فَيَكُونُ.

Classifications of Existence-Life

One should remember that in human classification of life, there are plants, animals and humans.

Yet, when Allah ﷻ mentions any being coming to existence such as stones, mountains, sky, sun, moon, or earth other than plants, animals and humans, these beings also have an identity and self in their relationship with Allah ﷻ.

In human classifications, "an organism represents a basic unit of life as an individual animal, plant, or single-celled life form" [1].

Then, "there is the microorganisms defined as a microscopic organism, especially a bacterium, virus, or fungus" [1].

For example,

> bacteria are a member of a large group of unicellular microorganisms that have cell walls but lack organelles and an organized nucleus, including some that can cause disease. Bacteria are widely distributed in soil, water, and air, and on or in the tissues of plants and animals. Formerly included in the plant kingdom, they are now classified separately (as prokaryotes). They play a vital role in global ecology, as the chemical changes they bring about include those of organic decay and nitrogen fixation.

Much modern biochemical knowledge has been gained from the study of bacteria because they grow easily and reproduce rapidly in laboratory cultures [1].

Then, "prokaryotes are named and classified as a microscopic single-celled organism that has neither a distinct nucleus with a membrane nor other specialized organelles. Prokaryotes include the bacteria and cyanobacteria" [1].

Cyanobacteria is named and classified as "a division of microorganisms that are related to the bacteria but are capable of photosynthesis. They are prokaryotic and represent the *earliest known form of life on the earth*" in today's human taxonomy [1].

Plants can be defined in today's classifications as

beings as a living organism of the kind exemplified by trees, shrubs, herbs, grasses, ferns, and mosses, typically growing in a permanent site, absorbing water and inorganic substances through its roots, and synthesizing nutrients in its leaves by photosynthesis using the green pigment chlorophyll. Plants differ from animals in lacking specialized sense organs, having no capacity for voluntary movement, having cell walls, and growing to suit their surroundings rather than having a fixed body plan, [1].

Animals are defined in today's classifications as

a living organism that feeds on organic matter, typically having specialized sense organs and nervous system and able to respond rapidly to stimuli. Animals are generally distinguished from plants by being unable to synthesize organic molecules from inorganic ones, so that they have to feed on plants or on other animals. They are typically able to move about, although this ability is sometimes restricted to a particular stage in the life cycle. The great majority of animals are invertebrates, of which there are some thirty phyla; the vertebrates constitute but a single subphylum. Animals are classified into higher and lower animals depending on their complexities in their bodies [1].

Humans are defined in today's classifications as "a man, woman, or child of the species Homo sapiens, distinguished from other beings by superior mental development, power of articulate speech, and upright stance" [1]. Homo in Latin means man and sapiens is wise. Homo sapiens is translated as wise man.

One should remember that as humans' scientific tools advance about the classification and terms determining basic unit of life or existence change, then it goes further into micro levels.

Yet, one should remember our previous discussion about atoms in their discussion of subatomic particles or levels, how or why they form the cells. These are some of the basic questions about the epistemology of classification of science that lack a satisfying answer before jumping into the complex classifications, taxonomies and groupings.

In this long journey of dabbling of definitions, and classifications of life and species, one should relax themselves and consult always the guidance of the Qurān and sunnah of Rasulullah ﷺ in seeking knowledge with the purpose, goal and intention of increasing one's imān and yaqìn in order to get closer to Allah ﷻ and please Allah ﷻ.

First and foremost, Allah ﷻ created everything and everything is mahkluq and they are in the realm of existence as mentioned repeatedly in the Quran:[15]

اللَّهُ الَّذِي خَلَقَ السَّمَاوَاتِ وَالْأَرْضَ وَمَا بَيْنَهُمَا فِي سِتَّةِ أَيَّامٍ ثُمَّ اسْتَوَى عَلَى الْعَرْشِ مَا لَكُم مِّن دُونِهِ مِن وَلِيٍّ وَلَا شَفِيعٍ أَفَلَا تَتَذَكَّرُونَ {السجدة/4}

هُوَ الَّذِي خَلَقَ السَّمَاوَاتِ وَالْأَرْضَ فِي سِتَّةِ أَيَّامٍ ثُمَّ اسْتَوَى عَلَى الْعَرْشِ يَعْلَمُ مَا يَلِجُ فِي الْأَرْضِ وَمَا يَخْرُجُ مِنْهَا وَمَا يَنزِلُ مِنَ السَّمَاءِ وَمَا يَعْرُجُ فِيهَا وَهُوَ مَعَكُمْ أَيْنَ مَا كُنتُمْ وَاللَّهُ بِمَا تَعْمَلُونَ بَصِيرٌ {الحديد/4}[16]

---

15. It is Allah who created the heavens and the earth and whatever is between them in six days; then He established Himself above the Throne. You have not besides Him any protector or any intercessor; so will you not be reminded?
16. It is He who created the heavens and earth in six days and then established Himself above the Throne. He knows what penetrates into the earth and what emerges from it and what descends from the heaven and what ascends therein; and He is with you wherever you are. And Allah, of what you do, is Seeing.

Yet, each being remember, Allah ﷻ in their tasbìh and dhikr as mentioned أَلَمْ تَرَ أَنَّ اللَّهَ يُسَبِّحُ لَهُ مَن فِي السَّمَاوَاتِ وَالْأَرْضِ وَالطَّيْرُ صَافَّاتٍ كُلٌّ قَدْ عَلِمَ صَلَاتَهُ وَتَسْبِيحَهُ وَاللَّهُ عَلِيمٌ بِمَا يَفْعَلُونَ {النور/41}[17]

In this categorization, these beings such as mountains, sky or earth have an identity to take position against the kufr of humans as mentioned:

تَكَادُ السَّمَاوَاتُ يَتَفَطَّرْنَ مِن فَوْقِهِنَّ وَالْمَلَائِكَةُ يُسَبِّحُونَ بِحَمْدِ رَبِّهِمْ وَيَسْتَغْفِرُونَ لِمَن فِي الْأَرْضِ أَلَا إِنَّ اللَّهَ هُوَ الْغَفُورُ الرَّحِيمُ {الشورى/5} وَالَّذِينَ اتَّخَذُوا مِن دُونِهِ أَوْلِيَاءَ اللَّهُ حَفِيظٌ عَلَيْهِمْ وَمَا أَنتَ عَلَيْهِم بِوَكِيلٍ {الشورى/6}[18]

They have position to choose or not as mentioned[19] إِنَّا عَرَضْنَا الْأَمَانَةَ عَلَى السَّمَاوَاتِ وَالْأَرْضِ وَالْجِبَالِ فَأَبَيْنَ أَن يَحْمِلْنَهَا وَأَشْفَقْنَ مِنْهَا وَحَمَلَهَا الْإِنسَانُ إِنَّهُ كَانَ ظَلُومًا جَهُولًا {الأحزاب/72}

In this categorization as mentioned in the Qurān and sunnah of Rasulullah ﷺ, everything has an identity and self once they become in existence as being regardless of their categorization of living-being, or non-living being, animate or in-animate beings.

First, since they are now in the realm of creation as mahlûq of Allah ﷻ, they primarily have the intrinsic property of gratitude, appreciation with tasbìh and hamd as mentioned[20]

هُوَ اللَّهُ الْخَالِقُ الْبَارِئُ الْمُصَوِّرُ لَهُ الْأَسْمَاء الْحُسْنَى يُسَبِّحُ لَهُ مَا فِي السَّمَاوَاتِ وَالْأَرْضِ وَهُوَ الْعَزِيزُ الْحَكِيمُ {الحشر/24}

أَلَمْ تَرَ أَنَّ اللَّهَ يُسَبِّحُ لَهُ مَن فِي السَّمَاوَاتِ وَالْأَرْضِ وَالطَّيْرُ صَافَّاتٍ كُلٌّ قَدْ عَلِمَ صَلَاتَهُ وَتَسْبِيحَهُ وَاللَّهُ عَلِيمٌ بِمَا يَفْعَلُونَ {النور/41}[21]

---

17. Do you not see that Allah is exalted by whomever is within the heavens and the earth and [by] the birds with wings spread [in flight]? Each [of them] has known his [means of] prayer and exalting [Him], and Allah is Knowing of what they do.

18. The heavens almost break from above them, and the angels exalt [Allah] with praise of their Lord and ask forgiveness for those on earth. Unquestionably, it is Allah who is the Forgiving, the Merciful. And those who take as allies other than Him - Allah is [yet] Guardian over them; and you, [O Muhammad], are not over them a manager.

19. Indeed, we offered the Trust to the heavens and the earth and the mountains, and they declined to bear it and feared it; but man [undertook to] bear it. Indeed, he was unjust and ignorant.

20. He is Allah, the Creator, the Inventor, the Fashioner; to Him belong the best names. Whatever is in the heavens and earth is exalting Him. And He is the Exalted in Might, the Wise..

21. Do you not see that Allah is exalted by whomever is within the heavens and the earth and [by] the birds with wings spread [in flight]? Each [of them] has known his [means of] prayer and exalting [Him], and Allah is Knowing of what they do.

وَتَرَى الْمَلَائِكَةَ حَافِّينَ مِنْ حَوْلِ الْعَرْشِ يُسَبِّحُونَ بِحَمْدِ رَبِّهِمْ وَقُضِيَ بَيْنَهُم بِالْحَقِّ وَقِيلَ الْحَمْدُ لِلَّهِ رَبِّ الْعَالَمِينَ {الزمر/75}[22]

They can even take positions about some of the ingratitude attitudes of some of the mahluq such as humans and Jinn when they lack this natural and fitri position of gratitude, appreciation with tasbhih and hamd as mentioned[23] تَكَادُ السَّمَاوَاتُ يَتَفَطَّرْنَ مِن فَوْقِهِنَّ وَالْمَلَائِكَةُ يُسَبِّحُونَ بِحَمْدِ رَبِّهِمْ وَيَسْتَغْفِرُونَ لِمَن فِي الْأَرْضِ أَلَا إِنَّ اللَّهَ هُوَ الْغَفُورُ الرَّحِيمُ {الشورى/5}

In this notion of beings beyond today's scientific classifications of living things and non-living things, one can remember the practice of Rasulullah ﷺ naming his ﷺ brush and items. One can remember the conversation of animals with Rasulullah ﷺ [2][24].

One can also remember the practice of Rasulullah ﷺ planting a flower or plant on a grave of person who was going through punishment of grave [3][25]. Due to the tasbih and dhikr of that plant on the grave, Allah ﷻ could relieve the person's punishment in the grave, that could be the hikmah, wisdom, Allahu A'lam.

In all above discussions, one can remember that once everything becomes in existence with the creation of Allah ﷻ, regardless of what it is, then everything has the natural and fitri state of tasbih and hamd with gratitude and hamd for Allah ﷻ.

Even for humans and jinn, in their initial creation stage as mentioned in qawlu bala, they had also the initial, natural, and fitri recognition of their Rabb, Allah ﷻ as mentioned[26] وَإِذْ أَخَذَ رَبُّكَ مِن بَنِي آدَمَ مِن ظُهُورِهِمْ ذُرِّيَّتَهُمْ وَأَشْهَدَهُمْ عَلَى أَنفُسِهِمْ أَلَسْتُ بِرَبِّكُمْ قَالُواْ بَلَى شَهِدْنَا أَن تَقُولُواْ يَوْمَ الْقِيَامَةِ إِنَّا كُنَّا عَنْ هَذَا غَافِلِينَ {الأعراف/172}. Yet, they forgot their initial promise at the incident

---

22. And you will see the angels surrounding the Throne, exalting [Allah] with praise of their Lord. And it will be judged between them in truth, and it will be said, "[All] praise to Allah, Lord of the worlds."

23. The heavens almost break from above them, and the angels exalt [Allah] with praise of their Lord and ask forgiveness for those on earth. Unquestionably, it is Allah who is the Forgiving, the Merciful.

24. Hadith #2549

25. Hadith #216

26. And [mention] when your Lord took from the children of Adam - from their loins - their descendants and made them testify of themselves, [saying to them], "Am I not your Lord?" They said, "Yes, we have testified." [This] - lest you should say on the day of Resurrection, "Indeed, we were of this unaware."

of qawlu – balā as mentioned[27] وَلَقَدْ عَهِدْنَا إِلَى آدَمَ مِن قَبْلُ فَنَسِيَ وَلَمْ نَجِدْ لَهُ عَزْمًا {طٰه/115}.

Yet, as the complexities increase with in these beings with movability, execution of order, bodies, and other intrinsic and extrinsic properties, Allah ﷻ offered a limited trial self-execution process of free-will to choose to fulfil a responsibility. Yet, all the beings were hesitant if they would be able to fulfil this responsibility. Yet humans and jinn acquired this free-will position as the claimant of Khalifah of Allah ﷻ on earth at a limited space and with a limited time of life span as a being implementing responsibilities on earth.

Once, they chose to be in that position then, they were sent to this world in the Divine Qadar of Allah ﷻ under the causalities of mother and father with a birth, growth and execution time and span of this free will until death.

Allah ﷻ in this execution time did not leave them without guidance. Allah ﷻ sent them the scriptures, the Qurān and the prophets, Rasulullah ﷺ.

Yet, in this execution some were successful, and some were not. Some adapted the guidance of Allah ﷻ with the Fadl and Karam of Allah ﷻ. Some did not adapt this guidance to reveal their initial intention of choice or push of being of human-being as the khalifah of Allah ﷻ on earth due to their arrogance. They forgot their initial promise at the incident of qawlu – balā as mentioned[28] وَلَقَدْ عَهِدْنَا إِلَى آدَمَ مِن قَبْلُ فَنَسِيَ وَلَمْ نَجِدْ لَهُ عَزْمًا {طٰه/115}. They lived a life of gaflah by forgetting this initial promise in qawlu-balā that they recognized their Creator, Rabbul Alamin and they would continue to be grateful with tasbìh and hamd in 'ibadah and now in action as the khalifah of Allah ﷻ on earth. Yet, this long-life forgetfulness called gaflah was the main attitude to reveal the attitudes of arrogance (astagfirullah) as mentioned:[29]

وَضَرَبَ لَنَا مَثَلًا وَنَسِيَ خَلْقَهُ قَالَ مَنْ يُحْيِي الْعِظَامَ وَهِيَ رَمِيمٌ {يٰس/78}

---

27. And We had already taken a promise from Adam before, but he forgot; and We found not in him determination.
28. And We had already taken a promise from Adam before, but he forgot; and We found not in him determination.
29. And he presents for Us an example and forgets his [own] creation. He says, "Who will give life to bones while they are disintegrated?"

فَذُوقُوا بِمَا نَسِيتُمْ لِقَاء يَوْمِكُمْ هَذَا إِنَّا نَسِينَاكُمْ وَذُوقُوا عَذَابَ الْخُلْدِ بِمَا كُنتُمْ تَعْمَلُونَ
{السجدة/14}[30]

وَقِيلَ الْيَوْمَ نَنسَاكُمْ كَمَا نَسِيتُمْ لِقَاء يَوْمِكُمْ هَذَا وَمَأْوَاكُمُ النَّارُ وَمَا لَكُم مِّن نَّاصِرِينَ
{الجاثية/34}[31]

الْمُنَافِقُونَ وَالْمُنَافِقَاتُ بَعْضُهُم مِّن بَعْضٍ يَأْمُرُونَ بِالْمُنكَرِ وَيَنْهَوْنَ عَنِ الْمَعْرُوفِ
وَيَقْبِضُونَ أَيْدِيَهُمْ نَسُواْ اللَّهَ فَنَسِيَهُمْ إِنَّ الْمُنَافِقِينَ هُمُ الْفَاسِقُونَ {التوبة/67}[32]

In the above types of forgetfulness, an attitude of permanent and by choice forgetfulness is the outcome of the attitude of arrogance. It is normal for humans to forget and we forget. Even, Rasulullah ﷺ taught us in the sajdah sahaw and mentioned for himself that as humans it is normal to forget, [2] (hadith 572#). Yet, this is the trial and test. Yet, once the person remembers the mistake, he or she does not ignore but try to do a make-up such as sajdah sahaw or tawba and istigfar to reconnect with Allah ﷻ.

As long as this is not deliberate, as soon as and as much as we try to ask forgiveness, and connect to Allah ﷻ with istigfar, tawba, ibadah and good deeds, this is a virtuous act. Yet, here the discussion is about the purposeful negligence and attitude of forgetfulness due to arrogance embodied by munafiq and kafir as mentioned[33] يَا أَيُّهَا الَّذِينَ آمَنُوا اتَّقُوا اللَّه

وَلْتَنظُرْ نَفْسٌ مَّا قَدَّمَتْ لِغَدٍ وَاتَّقُوا اللَّهَ إِنَّ اللَّهَ خَبِيرٌ بِمَا تَعْمَلُونَ {الحشر/18} وَلَا تَكُونُوا كَالَّذِينَ
نَسُوا اللَّهَ فَأَنسَاهُمْ أَنفُسَهُمْ أُوْلَئِكَ هُمُ الْفَاسِقُونَ {الحشر/19}

May Allah ﷻ protect us, Amìn.

In this regard, the goal of Shaytān is to increase the avenues of forgetfulness and ghaflah in the embodiment of remembrance of Allah

---

30. So taste [punishment] because you forgot the meeting of this, your Day; indeed, We have [accordingly] forgotten you. And taste the punishment of eternity for what you used to do."
31. And it will be said, "Today We will forget you as you forgot the meeting of this Day of yours, and your refuge is the Fire, and for you there are no helpers.
32. The hypocrite men and hypocrite women are of one another. They enjoin what is wrong and forbid what is right and close their hands. They have forgotten Allah, so He has forgotten them [accordingly]. Indeed, the hypocrites - it is they who are the defiantly disobedient.
33. O you who have believed, fear Allah. And let every soul look to what it has put forth for tomorrow - and fear Allah. Indeed, Allah is Acquainted with what you do. And be not like those who forgot Allah, so He made them forget themselves. Those are the defiantly disobedient.

قَالَ أَرَأَيْتَ إِذْ أَوَيْنَا إِلَى الصَّخْرَةِ فَإِنِّي نَسِيتُ الْحُوتَ وَمَا أَنْسَانِيهُ إِلَّا ۞ as mentioned[34]
الشَّيْطَانُ أَنْ أَذْكُرَهُ وَاتَّخَذَ سَبِيلَهُ فِي الْبَحْرِ عَجَبًا {الكهف/63}

This short life span of time and space differentiated the initial pool of the mixed of human and Jinn with different intentions coming to the earth. The short life span of time and span of earth revealed the ones with the initial intention of arrogance of superiority when they were offered the position of a being with free-will. These were the munafiqs and kafir.

Then, the ones who had the pure intention were separated from them who were the believers.

This separation reality is mentioned as[35] إِنَّا عَرَضْنَا الْأَمَانَةَ عَلَى السَّمَاوَاتِ
وَالْأَرْضِ وَالْجِبَالِ فَأَبَيْنَ أَنْ يَحْمِلْنَهَا وَأَشْفَقْنَ مِنْهَا وَحَمَلَهَا الْإِنْسَانُ إِنَّهُ كَانَ ظَلُومًا جَهُولًا
{الأحزاب/72} لِيُعَذِّبَ اللَّهُ الْمُنَافِقِينَ وَالْمُنَافِقَاتِ وَالْمُشْرِكِينَ وَالْمُشْرِكَاتِ وَيَتُوبَ اللَّهُ عَلَى
الْمُؤْمِنِينَ وَالْمُؤْمِنَاتِ وَكَانَ اللَّهُ غَفُورًا رَحِيمًا {الأحزاب/73}

In this regard of free will, the embodied arrogance was with Shaytān with the longest life span of time and space as mentioned[36] { قَالَ يَا إِبْلِيسُ
مَا مَنَعَكَ أَنْ تَسْجُدَ لِمَا خَلَقْتُ بِيَدَيَّ أَسْتَكْبَرْتَ أَمْ كُنْتَ مِنَ الْعَالِينَ {ص/75} قَالَ أَنَا خَيْرٌ مِنْهُ
خَلَقْتَنِي مِنْ نَارٍ وَخَلَقْتَهُ مِنْ طِينٍ {ص/76} قَالَ فَاخْرُجْ مِنْهَا فَإِنَّكَ رَجِيمٌ {ص/77} وَإِنَّ عَلَيْكَ
لَعْنَتِي إِلَى يَوْمِ الدِّينِ {ص/78} قَالَ رَبِّ فَأَنْظِرْنِي إِلَى يَوْمِ يُبْعَثُونَ {ص/79} قَالَ فَإِنَّكَ مِنَ
الْمُنْظَرِينَ {ص/80} إِلَى يَوْمِ الْوَقْتِ الْمَعْلُومِ {ص/81}.

The embodied humility and humbleness of being a'bd and true khalifah was revealed with Rasulullah ۞ as the role model for all creation in a short life span but with an unending effect as mentioned[37]
وَمَا أَرْسَلْنَاكَ إِلَّا رَحْمَةً لِّلْعَالَمِينَ {الأنبياء/107}.

Rabbana, La Tuzigh Qulubana Ba'da iz hadaytana wa hablana Rahmah innaka antal wahhab! Amìn,

---

34. He said, "Did you see when we retired to the rock? Indeed, I forgot [there] the fish. And none made me forget it except Satan - that I should mention it. And it took its course into the sea amazingly".
35. Indeed, we offered the Trust to the heavens and the earth and the mountains, and they declined to bear it and feared it; but man [undertook to] bear it. Indeed, he was unjust and ignorant. [It was] so that Allah may punish the hypocrite men and hypocrite women and the men and women who associate others with Him and that Allah may accept repentance from the believing men and believing women. And ever is Allah Forgiving and Merciful.
36. [Allah] said, "O Iblees, what prevented you from prostrating to that which I created with My hands? Were you arrogant [then], or were you [already] among the haughty?" He said, "I am better than him. You created me from fire and created him from clay." [Allah] said, "Then get out of Paradise, for indeed, you are expelled. And indeed, upon you is My curse until the Day of Recompense." He said, "My Lord, then reprieve me until the Day they are resurrected." [Allah] said, "So indeed, you are of those reprieved Until the Day of the time well-known."
37. And We have not sent you, [O Muhammad], except as a mercy to the worlds.

Rabbana, Ajalna attitbu' sunnata Habibuka 🌸, imamana 🌸, rasuluna saw, wa mawlana 🌸 , Amìn,

May Allah 🌸 protect us from forgetting Allah 🌸 in our short span of life time and space, Amìn

May Allah 🌸 make us to be in constant dhikr, tasbìh, hamd of Allah 🌸 in attitude and ibadah as we were initially created for and make us embody the amalu salih and good actions with the Dhikrullah to please Allah 🌸 as trying to fulfil the responsibility of being khalifah of Allah 🌸 through the guidance of the Qurãn and Sunnah of Rasulullah 🌸.

Allahumma Salli ala sayyidina wa habibana Muhammad 🌸 Amìn.

Qualities of Life and Existence

One should realize that existence and life is one of the highest, sensitive and mystical miracles of Allah 🌸. Life and existence is the highest ni'mah of Allah 🌸 given to all beings. Life and existence is in its all qualities is the most clear proof for Allah 🌸.

Humans have very limited knowledge since the beginning of creation about the real quality of life and existence as mentioned with the word rûh in[38] وَيَسْأَلُونَكَ عَنِ الرُّوحِ قُلِ الرُّوحُ مِنْ أَمْرِ رَبِّي وَمَا أُوتِيتُم مِّنَ الْعِلْمِ إِلَّا قَلِيلًا. {الإسراء/85}

After a thing is in existence with the Divine Mashiyyah, Will of Allah 🌸 and that thing comes into existence as a being, then one can mention about the existence of that being and name them and try to identify them with its, his or her qualities and details.

One of the identifiable and differentiating factors among beings is their observable ability to move.

Yes, one of the classical and present taxonomy of humans of beings is based on the movability of beings in their classification such as plants, animals or humans.

Yet, through the analysis of the Qurãn, one should analyze and try to approach and extrapolate the true and real meanings of things as outlined by Allah 🌸 and in the practices of Rasulullah 🌸.

---

38. And they ask you, [O Muhammad], about the soul. Say, "The soul is of the affair of my Lord. And mankind have not been given of knowledge except a little."

Degrees of Freedom: The Quality of Movability

Allah ﷻ has given the ability of moving to the beings. This can be one of the qualities of existence and life.

This freedom of movability can be different for different beings.

This movability can be intrinsic and involuntary as established by Allah ﷻ. This movability can be extrinsic and voluntary with some limited freedom as bestowed by Allah ﷻ.

This movability can be intrinsic and involuntary movability in their bodies such as the blood flowing in circular systems or the dynamics of action a cell through its mechanisms such as mitochondria, nucleus or membrane as established by Allah SWT. Even, there can be an argument at subatomic levels of electrons, protons or neutrons how this movability at that level or lower levels are signs of beings as established by Allah SWT.

This movability can be extrinsic and voluntary and/involuntary with some limited freedom as bestowed by Allah ﷻ. The limited freedom of movability for a plant can be through the branching of its roots under the soil and spreading. It can be also branching of its upper torso with its fruits and spreading towards the sky vertically and in the sky horizontally. One can consider a date tree and sidr tree. One going up and the other going vertically. SubhanAllah! As everything is a sign and ayah from Allah ﷻ, the shape of these trees in their tendencies show us how and what to be in our relationship with Allah ﷻ.

The limited freedom of movability for an animal can be very vast with its categorization of feet as mentioned in the Qurān[39] وَاللَّهُ خَلَقَ كُلَّ دَابَّةٍ مِن مَّاء فَمِنْهُم مَّن يَمْشِي عَلَى بَطْنِهِ وَمِنْهُم مَّن يَمْشِي عَلَى رِجْلَيْنِ وَمِنْهُم مَّن يَمْشِي عَلَى أَرْبَعٍ يَخْلُقُ اللَّهُ مَا يَشَاء إِنَّ اللَّهَ عَلَى كُلِّ شَيْءٍ قَدِيرٌ {النور /45}.

Some can fly such as the bees and birds.

Some can walk and jump such as the cats, and insects.

Some can crawl or move such as the snakes and bacteria.

Depending on their physical movability, they can have the freedom of life and they can have the freedom of interacting with the nature and universe as created and established by Allah ﷻ. Even, mathematicians use a term for degrees of freedom [1].

---

39. Allah has created every [living] creature from water. And of them are those that move on their bellies, and of them are those that walk on two legs, and of them are those that walk on four. Allah creates what He wills. Indeed, Allah is over all things competent.

In this case, one can remember the classical definition of degrees of freedom in physics as a direction in which independent motion can occur [1].

Our goal here is to remind the reader the connection and complexity of life and existence through the notion of technical terms as already present in basics math, physics and even chemistry today.

Now, one can connect the notion of movability given to beings in their degrees of freedom and their free-will if or how this movability is related.

Degrees of Freedom: The Quality of Intellect & Free Will

For all beings, Allah ﷻ inspires them and they do what they do and in their intrinsic and embedded trained knowledge as given by Allah ﷻ. One can remember the honeybee as mentioned in the Qurān and the word wahiy-inspiration is used as mentioned[40] وَأَوْحَى رَبُّكَ إِلَى النَّحْلِ أَنِ اتَّخِذِي مِنَ الْجِبَالِ بُيُوتًا وَمِنَ الشَّجَرِ وَمِمَّا يَعْرِشُونَ {النحل/68}

On the other hand, beings can have will and logic even what we call them as inanimate as mentioned, for example an ant:[41]

حَتَّى إِذَا أَتَوْا عَلَى وَادِي النَّمْلِ قَالَتْ نَمْلَةٌ يَا أَيُّهَا النَّمْلُ ادْخُلُوا مَسَاكِنَكُمْ لَا يَحْطِمَنَّكُمْ سُلَيْمَانُ وَجُنُودُهُ وَهُمْ لَا يَشْعُرُونَ {النمل/18}

A bird in her critical thinking and argumentation, and free will of being delayed while under the command of Sulayman as:[42]

مَا لِيَ لَا أَرَى الْهُدْهُدَ أَمْ كَانَ مِنَ الْغَائِبِينَ {النمل/20} لَأُعَذِّبَنَّهُ عَذَابًا شَدِيدًا أَوْ لَأَذْبَحَنَّهُ أَوْ لَيَأْتِيَنِّي بِسُلْطَانٍ مُبِينٍ {النمل/21} فَمَكَثَ غَيْرَ بَعِيدٍ فَقَالَ أَحَطتُ بِمَا لَمْ تُحِطْ بِهِ وَجِئْتُكَ مِن سَبَإٍ بِنَبَإٍ يَقِينٍ {النمل/22}

---

40. And your Lord inspired to the bee, "Take for yourself among the mountains, houses, and among the trees and [in] that which they construct.
41. Until, when they came upon the valley of the ants, an ant said, "O ants, enter your dwellings that you not be crushed by Solomon and his soldiers while they perceive not."
42. And he took attendance of the birds and said, "Why do I not see the hoopoe - or is he among the absent? I will surely punish him with a severe punishment or slaughter him unless he brings me clear authorization."

إِنِّي وَجَدتُ امْرَأَةً تَمْلِكُهُمْ وَأُوتِيَتْ مِن كُلِّ شَيْءٍ وَلَهَا عَرْشٌ عَظِيمٌ {النمل/23}[43] وَجَدتُّهَا وَقَوْمَهَا يَسْجُدُونَ لِلشَّمْسِ مِن دُونِ اللَّهِ وَزَيَّنَ لَهُمُ الشَّيْطَانُ أَعْمَالَهُمْ فَصَدَّهُمْ عَنِ السَّبِيلِ فَهُمْ لَا يَهْتَدُونَ {النمل/24} أَلَّا يَسْجُدُوا لِلَّهِ الَّذِي يُخْرِجُ الْخَبْءَ فِي السَّمَاوَاتِ وَالْأَرْضِ وَيَعْلَمُ مَا تُخْفُونَ وَمَا تُعْلِنُونَ {النمل/25} اللَّهُ لَا إِلَهَ إِلَّا هُوَ رَبُّ الْعَرْشِ الْعَظِيمِ {النمل/26}

For example, a sky and earth[44]

ثُمَّ اسْتَوَى إِلَى السَّمَاء وَهِيَ دُخَانٌ فَقَالَ لَهَا وَلِلْأَرْضِ ائْتِيَا طَوْعًا أَوْ كَرْهًا قَالَتَا أَتَيْنَا طَائِعِينَ {فصلت/11}

In this sense, Allah ﷻ give the life from non-existence into existence. When they become existence, these beings have life, some intellect and free-will as mentioned in the above ayahs.

When Rasulullah ﷺ ordered the mountain Uhud to stop shaking when Rasulullah ﷺ, Abu Bakir ra, Omar ra and Osman ra were all on them [4][45].

Seed of Kufr in Today's Scientific Classifications of Living Things and Non-Living Things

In this regard, the present or modern classification of science as living things or non-living things really fail. This is not according to the understanding of the Qurān, Sunnah of Rasulullah ﷺ and perspectives of imān.

Even if the current science categorizes the things related with life according to their movability or not, they still fail in that categorization. Mountains according to the current classification is stationary, not moving. Yet, the Qurān mentions that[46] وَتَرَى الْجِبَالَ تَحْسَبُهَا جَامِدَةً وَهِيَ تَمُرُّ مَرَّ السَّحَابِ صُنْعَ اللَّهِ الَّذِي أَتْقَنَ كُلَّ شَيْءٍ إِنَّهُ خَبِيرٌ بِمَا تَفْعَلُونَ {النمل/88}.

---

43. Indeed, I found [there] a woman ruling them, and she has been given of all things, and she has a great throne. I found her and her people prostrating to the sun instead of Allah, and Satan has made their deeds pleasing to them and averted them from [His] way, so they are not guided, [And] so they do not prostrate to Allah, who brings forth what is hidden within the heavens and the earth and knows what you conceal and what you declare - Allah - there is no deity except Him, Lord of the Great Throne."
44. Then He directed Himself to the heaven while it was smoke and said to it and to the earth, "Come [into being], willingly or by compulsion." They said, "We have come willingly."
45. Hadith #3699
46. And you see the mountains, thinking them rigid, while they will pass as the passing of clouds. [It is] the work of Allah, who perfected all things. Indeed, He is Acquainted with that which you do.

The darkness of kufr in the implementation of secularism identify, tag, interpret and popularize terms that plant the seeds of kufr, and darkness that we don't really understand. IN other words, excluding Allah ﷻ, in each sentence of scientific discovery implants a seed of kufr regardless of the greatness of the discovery and invention, SubhanAllah!

Yet, all these beings in their natural fitri stance of being mahluq of Allah ﷻ, still constantly remember and make dhikr, tasbih and show gratitude and appreciation to Allah ﷻ as mentioned[47] أَلَمْ تَرَ أَنَّ الله يُسَبِّحُ لَهُ مَن فِي السَّمَاوَاتِ وَالْأَرْضِ وَالطَّيْرُ صَافَّاتٍ كُلٌّ قَدْ عَلِمَ صَلَاتَهُ وَتَسْبِيحَهُ وَاللَّهُ عَلِيمٌ بِمَا يَفْعَلُونَ {النور/41}.

Degrees of Freedom: Unique Position of Human Beings and Jinn in Free Will and Intellect

If we consider human beings and Jinn, they have the degrees of freedom through their physical means and also through their aqil, intellect/logic and basirah, true experience/emotions or some can call this basirah as wijdān-conscience.

The movability of humans through their intellect, knowledge, I'lm and science can be so vast that they can travel faster than the speed of light through understanding and detailing the intricacies of everything in the universe. The ayah can indicate this superior quality of humans given to them as mentioned[48] وَلَقَدْ كَرَّمْنَا بَنِي آدَمَ وَحَمَلْنَاهُمْ فِي الْبَرِّ وَالْبَحْرِ وَرَزَقْنَاهُم مِّنَ الطَّيِّبَاتِ وَفَضَّلْنَاهُمْ عَلَى كَثِيرٍ مِّمَّنْ خَلَقْنَا تَفْضِيلاً {الإسراء/70}

Yet, on the other hand, humans and Jinn have a free-will pool either inspired by guidance of Allah ﷻ through the Qurān and Sunnah of Rasululah ﷺ, and/or tempted by their own raw ego/nafs and Shaytān.

In this existence of the highest quality of freedom of movability through intellect and I'lm has the counterbalancing agent of temptations of shaytan and nafs.

In this battle, humans have free-will either to enjoy the sweetness of iman and target the highest level in their proximity of taqwa with Allah ﷻ in this life or afterlife.

---

47. Do you not see that Allah is exalted by whomever is within the heavens and the earth and [by] the birds with wings spread [in flight]? Each [of them] has known his [means of] prayer and exalting [Him], and Allah is Knowing of what they do.

48. And We have certainly honored the children of Adam and carried them on the land and sea and provided for them of the good things and preferred them over much of what We have created, with [definite] preference.

Or, they can be worse than all the beings as mentioned in their degrees of freedom dragged behind their temptations of Shaytān and nafs and ignoring all the signs showering on the person about the reality of the dysfunction the a'qil and intellect.

That is the difference of an amanah. All the beings did not want to take the risk of displeasing Allah ﷻ by acquiring higher positions of degrees of freedom through higher levels of aqil, intellect, and free will as mentioned[49] إِنَّا عَرَضْنَا الْأَمَانَةَ عَلَى السَّمَاوَاتِ وَالْأَرْضِ وَالْجِبَالِ فَأَبَيْنَ أَن يَحْمِلْنَهَا وَأَشْفَقْنَ مِنْهَا وَحَمَلَهَا الْإِنسَانُ إِنَّهُ كَانَ ظَلُومًا جَهُولًا {الأحزاب/72}.

In this regard, one can possibly deduce that all the beings can have a type of intellect, and free will in different degrees of life and existence. One can review the above ayahs about the mountains, ant, and bird-Hud Hud in Sûrah Naml, and incidents at the time of Rasulullah ﷺ such as the complaining of a donkey about its owner and crying pillar in the masjid of Rasulullah ﷺ due to being distanced from Rasulullah 4] ﷺ][50]. Then, one can revisit these discussions of intellect, and free will in their different degrees of life and existence.

The Battle Between Shaytān and Humans: Substance vs Knowledge

Yet, humans including Jinn are given a higher level of degrees of freedoms as a test and trial through knowledge, ilm, and science. One can remember the ayahs as[51]

قَالَ عِفْرِيتٌ مِّنَ الْجِنِّ أَنَا آتِيكَ بِهِ قَبْلَ أَن تَقُومَ مِن مَّقَامِكَ وَإِنِّي عَلَيْهِ لَقَوِيٌّ أَمِينٌ {النمل/39}

قَالَ الَّذِي عِندَهُ عِلْمٌ مِّنَ الْكِتَابِ أَنَا آتِيكَ بِهِ قَبْلَ أَن يَرْتَدَّ إِلَيْكَ طَرْفُكَ فَلَمَّا رَآهُ مُسْتَقِرًّا عِندَهُ قَالَ هَذَا مِن فَضْلِ رَبِّي لِيَبْلُوَنِي أَأَشْكُرُ أَمْ أَكْفُرُ وَمَن شَكَرَ فَإِنَّمَا يَشْكُرُ لِنَفْسِهِ وَمَن كَفَرَ فَإِنَّ رَبِّي غَنِيٌّ كَرِيمٌ {النمل/40}[52].

---

49. Indeed, we offered the Trust to the heavens and the earth and the mountains, and they declined to bear it and feared it; but man [undertook to] bear it. Indeed, he was unjust and ignorant.

50. Hadith #3584

51. A powerful one from among the jinn said, "I will bring it to you before you rise from your place, and indeed, I am for this [task] strong and trustworthy."

52. Said one who had knowledge from the Scripture, "I will bring it to you before your glance returns to you." And when [Solomon] saw it placed before him, he said, "This is from the favor of my Lord to test me whether I will be grateful or ungrateful. And whoever is grateful - his gratitude is only for [the benefit of] himself. And whoever is ungrateful - then indeed, my Lord is Free of need and Generous."

The above ayah can indicate the power of ilm, knowledge and intellect. Even this ayah can indicate the overpowering higher level of degree of freedom of humans as قَالَ الَّذِي عِنْدَهُ عِلْمٌ over jinn as mentioned قَالَ عِفْرِيتٌ مِّنَ الْجِنِّ who can claim to the be better due to their physical overpowering over humans as mentioned by Shaytān[53] قَالَ أَنَا خَيْرٌ مِّنْهُ خَلَقْتَنِي مِن نَّارٍ وَخَلَقْتَهُ مِن طِينٍ {ص/76}.

This itself can prove physical or substantial quality of ranking is not a deserving ranking quality over the I'lm and knowledge in the comparison of قَالَ عِفْرِيتٌ مِّنَ الْجِنِّ and قَالَ الَّذِي عِنْدَهُ عِلْمٌ as claimed by Shaytān قَالَ أَنَا خَيْرٌ مِّنْهُ خَلَقْتَنِي مِن نَّارٍ وَخَلَقْتَهُ مِن طِينٍ {ص/76} as.

Another ayah as[54]

وَإِذْ قَالَ رَبُّكَ لِلْمَلَائِكَةِ إِنِّي جَاعِلٌ فِي الْأَرْضِ خَلِيفَةً قَالُوا أَتَجْعَلُ فِيهَا مَن يُفْسِدُ فِيهَا وَيَسْفِكُ الدِّمَاء وَنَحْنُ نُسَبِّحُ بِحَمْدِكَ وَنُقَدِّسُ لَكَ قَالَ إِنِّي أَعْلَمُ مَا لاَ تَعْلَمُونَ {البقرة/30} وَعَلَّمَ آدَمَ الأَسْمَاء كُلَّهَا ثُمَّ عَرَضَهُمْ عَلَى الْمَلاَئِكَةِ فَقَالَ أَنبِئُونِي بِأَسْمَاء هَؤُلاء إِن كُنتُمْ صَادِقِينَ {البقرة/31} قَالُواْ سُبْحَانَكَ لاَ عِلْمَ لَنَا إِلاَّ مَا عَلَّمْتَنَا إِنَّكَ أَنتَ الْعَلِيمُ الْحَكِيمُ {البقرة/32} قَالَ يَا آدَمُ أَنبِئْهُم بِأَسْمَآئِهِمْ فَلَمَّا أَنبَأَهُمْ بِأَسْمَآئِهِمْ قَالَ أَلَمْ أَقُل لَّكُمْ إِنِّي أَعْلَمُ غَيْبَ السَّمَاوَاتِ وَالأَرْضِ وَأَعْلَمُ مَا تُبْدُونَ وَمَا كُنتُمْ تَكْتُمُونَ {البقرة/33}

Allah ﷻ mentions in the above ayahs give the gist of the higher degrees of freedoms of humans in intellect, ilm and knowledge even over the angels. This higher degree of freedom in I'lm can make the humans use their higher degree of freedom in free-will on the earth as the khalifah of Allah ﷻ to fulfill the real purpose of their existence. Yet, some misuse this freedom and some fulfill it. Allahumma Ja'lana attabiu sunnata Muhammadan ﷺ, Amìn,

Even, one can view the thirst of Musa as about knowledge and I'lm in the realities of knowledge beyond the visible of alam shadah

53. He said, "I am better than him. You created me from fire and created him from clay."
54. And [mention, O Muhammad], when your Lord said to the angels, "Indeed, I will make upon the earth a successive authority." They said, "Will You place upon it one who causes corruption therein and sheds blood, while we declare Your praise and sanctify You?" Allah said, "Indeed, I know that which you do not know." And He taught Adam the names - all of them. Then He showed them to the angels and said, "Inform Me of the names of these, if you are truthful." They said, "Exalted are You; we have no knowledge except what You have taught us. Indeed, it is You who is the Knowing, the Wise." He said, "O Adam, inform them of their names." And when he had informed them of their names, He said, "Did I not tell you that I know the unseen [aspects] of the heavens and the earth? And I know what you reveal and what you have concealed."

can indicate this high position of humans in their degree of freedom embodied by one the prophets of Allah ﷻ as[55]

فَوَجَدَا عَبْدًا مِّنْ عِبَادِنَا آتَيْنَاهُ رَحْمَةً مِنْ عِندِنَا وَعَلَّمْنَاهُ مِن لَّدُنَّا عِلْمًا {الكهف/65} قَالَ لَهُ مُوسَى هَلْ أَتَّبِعُكَ عَلَى أَن تُعَلِّمَنِ مِمَّا عُلِّمْتَ رُشْدًا {الكهف/66}

Therefore, one can understand the higher degrees of freedom through knowledge and free-will given to humans by Allah ﷻ can be viewed in this ayah as[56] وَلَقَدْ كَرَّمْنَا بَنِي آدَمَ وَحَمَلْنَاهُمْ فِي الْبَرِّ وَالْبَحْرِ وَرَزَقْنَاهُم مِّنَ الطَّيِّبَاتِ وَفَضَّلْنَاهُمْ عَلَى كَثِيرٍ مِّمَّنْ خَلَقْنَا تَفْضِيلاً {الإسراء/70}

In all these above discussions, one can remember the possibilities of movability in all beings whether it is observable or not by humans.

This is a separate possibility for all the beings who have different degrees of freedom in life, existence, intellect and free will. On the other hand, humans and Jinn are given a specialized higher degree of freedom in life, existence, intellect and free will who can govern all the other beings as a test and trial. At the end of this trial, test or business, some become closer with taqwa in proximity to Allah ﷻ and some become distanced from Allah ﷻ due to their arrogance.

May Allah ﷻ protect us, Amìn.

Ilm-Knowledge & Its Reflection Experience-Emotions

One should remember that when one travels in the universe with knowledge, ilm, aqil and intellect, it is similar to being a guest in a house. A person goes to stars with knowledge, experiments and science through astrophysics and astronomy. A person goes to the darkness of the oceans trying to observe sleeping fish and sea plants knowledge, experiments and science through oceanography.

Yet, as the person visits all these different creation of Allah ﷻ, and incidents beyond time, past or future, these visitations require the ones who are visited to also visit this person.

---

55. And they found a servant from among Our servants to whom we had given mercy from us and had taught him from Us a [certain] knowledge. Moses said to him, "May I follow you on [the condition] that you teach me from what you have been taught of sound judgement?"
56. And We have certainly honored the children of Adam and carried them on the land and sea and provided for them of the good things and preferred them over much of what We have created, with [definite] preference.

The images, emotions, and experiences that we have after these visitations through aqil are visitors in our house of heart, qalb from them.

Therefore, if a person wants good visitors then, they should choose who to visit and why to visit. If a person visits the planet Mars with the intention of increasing one's imān, then the person can be visited by the guest of Mars in sajdah about the Azamah of Allah ﷻ increasing one's imān, yaqìn and certainty in five daily prayers, nawāfil and tahajjud. SubhanAllah!

On the other hand, if a person visits an incident promoting jealousy and hatred, then that incident can visit the person in the middle of night, making the person lose his or her sleep and putting the person in agitation, stress, and anxiety.

May Allah ﷻ make all our visits for the pleasure of Allah ﷻ increasing our imān, mārifah and yaqìn, Amìn.

Rental Universe: Beings and their Relationships

One should ponder about any being and its relationship with universe. If we consider a honeybee, traveling around different flowers, plants, valleys, and mountains, this honeybee can consider that all these other beings that it visits is created by Allah ﷻ for this honeybee. This honeybee even can claim that all the universe is created for this honeybee for its purpose.

Any being either a honeybee, a stone, a mountain, a tree, a cloud, an animal and humans, they all have relationships with their surroundings according to their degrees of freedom.

Yet, as discussed before, humans have the highest level of degrees of freedom in their relationship with other beings. Therefore, khalìfah can entail the meaning of this degree of freedom of humans overpowering justly or unjustly on other beings.

This overpowering of humans in an evil way over the other beings is called fasad or mischief as mentioned[57] ظَهَرَ الْفَسَادُ فِي الْبَرِّ وَالْبَحْرِ بِمَا كَسَبَتْ أَيْدِي النَّاسِ لِيُذِيقَهُم بَعْضَ الَّذِي عَمِلُوا لَعَلَّهُمْ يَرْجِعُونَ {الروم/41}.

---

57. Corruption has appeared throughout the land and sea by [reason of] what the hands of people have earned so He may let them taste part of [the consequence of] what they have done that perhaps they will return [to

This engagement of humans in evil or fasad through their degrees of freedom can desire such evils that they may want to eliminate the main purpose of existence and life with the Dhikrullah and ihsān accordingly doing amal-u salih with ihsān but Allah ﷻ does not allow with Divine Intervention the removal of this essential for existence as mentioned[58] الَّذِينَ أُخْرِجُوا مِن دِيَارِهِم بِغَيْرِ حَقٍّ إِلَّا أَن يَقُولُوا رَبُّنَا اللَّهُ وَلَوْلَا دَفْعُ اللَّهِ النَّاسَ بَعْضَهُم بِبَعْضٍ لَّهُدِّمَتْ صَوَامِعُ وَبِيَعٌ وَصَلَوَاتٌ وَمَسَاجِدُ يُذْكَرُ فِيهَا اسْمُ اللَّهِ كَثِيرًا وَلَيَنصُرَنَّ اللَّهُ مَن يَنصُرُهُ إِنَّ اللَّهَ لَقَوِيٌّ عَزِيزٌ {الحج/40}. This is the sunnatullah.

Yet, when Allah ﷻ allows this essential to be removed on the earth, then that is the time for End of Days.

Therefore, the institutions of remembrance of Allah ﷻ, as the Dhikrullah, in ibadah and amal at an individual level or collective level is considered in sunnatullah as a means for the Divine Protection. This is mentioned as[59] وَمَا كَانَ اللَّهُ لِيُعَذِّبَهُمْ وَأَنتَ فِيهِمْ وَمَا كَانَ اللَّهُ مُعَذِّبَهُمْ وَهُمْ يَسْتَغْفِرُونَ {الأنفال/33}. The highest form of Dhikrullah is the one that is following the sunnah of Rasulullah ﷺ.

Yet, in all these engagements, each being has a limited life span. Universe is constituted with all beings. Therefore, universe has a limited life span as the End of Day or Yawmul Qiyamah can indicate this reality.

Therefore, Allah ﷻ mentions in the Qurān to possibly emphasize and teach us this reality of temporality as[60] وَنُفِخَ فِي الصُّورِ فَصَعِقَ مَن فِي السَّمَاوَاتِ وَمَن فِي الْأَرْضِ إِلَّا مَن شَاءَ اللَّهُ ثُمَّ نُفِخَ فِيهِ أُخْرَى فَإِذَا هُم قِيَامٌ يَنظُرُونَ {الزمر/68}

وَيَوْمَ يُنفَخُ فِي الصُّورِ فَفَزِعَ مَن فِي السَّمَاوَاتِ وَمَن فِي الْأَرْضِ إِلَّا مَن شَاءَ اللَّهُ وَكُلٌّ أَتَوْهُ دَاخِرِينَ {النمل/87}[61]

One of the possible wisdoms of the incident of everything visible or invisible dying is that we do not attach ourselves in its true reality and

---

58. [They are] those who have been evicted from their homes without right - only because they say, "Our Lord is Allah." And were it not that Allah checks the people, some by means of others, there would have been demolished monasteries, churches, synagogues, and mosques in which the name of Allah is much mentioned. And Allah will surely support those who support Him. Indeed, Allah is Powerful and Exalted in Might.
59. But Allah would not punish them while you, [O Muhammad], are among them, and Allah would not punish them while they seek forgiveness.
60. And the Horn will be blown, and whoever is in the heavens and whoever is on the earth will fall dead except whom Allah wills. Then it will be blown again, and at once they will be standing, looking on.
61. And [warn of] the Day the Horn will be blown, and whoever is in the heavens and whoever is on the earth will be terrified except whom Allah wills. And all will come to Him humbled.

absoluteness except to Allah ﷻ. La ilaha illa Allah is the reality of this reality.

Everything is temporal even this universe, angels, galaxies, and all visible and invisible, mysterious or obvious beings except Allah ﷻ.

Allah ﷻ is the Permanent, Everlasting, Without any Beginning and End, the Creator, the Sustainer, the Maintainer of all systems, universes and structures.

Yet, Allah ﷻ is the Most Merciful, Ar-Rahman, Ar-Rahim, the Most Graceful, the Most Loving.

Therefore, once Allah ﷻ creates a being from non-existence into existence and life, there is the continuity of the existence and life due the Rahmah, Karam, Fadl of Allah ﷻ, Rabbul A'lamìn.

Our pious salaf all clearly stated in the light of the Qurān and sunnah that the existence of humans will continue in the afterlife in different abodes either in Jannah or Jahannam, May Allah ﷻ protect us. Yet, there are were some difference of opinion about the other beings' state after they die in life.

One should remember that a person can a have a pseudo-ownership referred as rental in today's terms. The position of human beings as Khalìfah is nothing more than a pseudo-ownership about the judgment and accountability of the person in front of Rabbul Alamin, if this person fulfilled played this role of being Khalìfah justly and properly, while on the earth in the temporary life span of the rental of the universe.

Life and existence can transform a miniscule and trivial looking thing into something important and very critical. All the beings with life and existence can declare that "this universe is mine." In their declaration and engagement with universe, the beings with life and existence do not have any conflicts. Only humans have conflicts, mischief and fasād in their claims of ownership as also declared by angels for humans as[62] وَإِذْ

قَالَ رَبُّكَ لِلْمَلاَئِكَةِ إِنِّي جَاعِلٌ فِي الأَرْضِ خَلِيفَةً قَالُواْ أَتَجْعَلُ فِيهَا مَن يُفْسِدُ فِيهَا وَيَسْفِكُ الدِّمَاء

وَنَحْنُ نُسَبِّحُ بِحَمْدِكَ وَنُقَدِّسُ لَكَ قَالَ إِنِّي أَعْلَمُ مَا لاَ تَعْلَمُونَ {البقرة/30}

---

62. And [mention, O Muhammad], when your Lord said to the angels, "Indeed, I will make upon the earth a successive authority." They said, "Will You place upon it one who causes corruption therein and sheds blood, while we declare Your praise and sanctify You?" Allah said, "Indeed, I know that which you do not know."

Life & Existence for Discoveries of Names and Attributes of Allah ﷻ

Allah ﷻ is beyond from all the similarities and examples, SubhanAllah!

When we consider one of the possible hikmahs-wisdoms of life and existence is that life and existence is the means to discover the realities of different Names and Attributes of Allah ﷻ reflected on different beings and creations.

In other words, when a being with life and existence discovers other beings with their life and existence, each being that they discover have different Names and Attributes of Allah ﷻ reflected on this being.

In the above section of rental universe, when a honeybee discovers flowers, plants and other beings in its travel with its degree of freedom, there are Names and Attributes of Allah ﷻ reflected on both the discoverer, the honeybee and the discovered being, the flower.

Depending on their degrees of freedom and capacity, each being remember and make tasbîh of Allah ﷻ in different forms and pray to Allah ﷻ and they are aware and conscious of their tasbîh and salah-prayers as mentioned[63] أَلَمْ تَرَ أَنَّ اللهَ يُسَبِّحُ لَهُ مَن فِي السَّمَاوَاتِ وَالْأَرْضِ وَالطَّيْرُ صَافَّاتٍ كُلٌّ قَدْ عَلِمَ صَلَاتَهُ وَتَسْبِيحَهُ وَاللهُ عَلِيمٌ بِمَا يَفْعَلُونَ {النور/41}. The expression كُلٌّ قَدْ عَلِمَ صَلَاتَهُ وَتَسْبِيحَهُ rejects some modern theological approaches that these beings unconsciously automated or involuntary way of making tasbîh or salah-prayers. No. They consciously know and aware of the tasbîh, salah and dhikr of Allah ﷻ and this is a natural state similarly to air inhaling of humans. Yet, they love it and they cannot be in life and existence without the remembrance of Allah ﷻ, Dhikrullah.

When humans discover other beings in the universe through science, ilm, knowledge according to their degrees of freedom of free-will and a'qil-intellect, there are the Names and Attributes of Allah ﷻ reflected on both the discoverer, humans and the discovered being universe.

In this discovery of degrees of freedom, Allah ﷻ gave a higher allowance of degrees of freedom to humans as mentioned[64] وَإِذْ قَالَ رَبُّكَ

---

63. Do you not see that Allah is exalted by whomever is within the heavens and the earth and [by] the birds with wings spread [in flight]? Each [of them] has known his [means of] prayer and exalting [Him], and Allah is Knowing of what they do.

64. And [mention, O Muhammad], when your Lord said to the angels, "Indeed, I will make upon the earth a successive authority." They said, "Will You place upon it one who causes corruption therein and sheds blood, while we declare Your praise and sanctify You?" Allah said, "Indeed, I know that which you do not know." And He taught Adam the names - all of them. Then He showed them to the angels and said, "Inform Me of the names of these, if you are truthful."

لِلْمَلَائِكَةِ إِنِّي جَاعِلٌ فِي الْأَرْضِ خَلِيفَةً قَالُوا أَتَجْعَلُ فِيهَا مَن يُفْسِدُ فِيهَا وَيَسْفِكُ الدِّمَاءَ وَنَحْنُ نُسَبِّحُ بِحَمْدِكَ وَنُقَدِّسُ لَكَ قَالَ إِنِّي أَعْلَمُ مَا لَا تَعْلَمُونَ {البقرة/30} وَعَلَّمَ آدَمَ الْأَسْمَاءَ كُلَّهَا ثُمَّ عَرَضَهُمْ عَلَى الْمَلَائِكَةِ فَقَالَ أَنبِئُونِي بِأَسْمَاءِ هَؤُلَاءِ إِن كُنتُمْ صَادِقِينَ {البقرة/31}.

Yet, one should remember that when true I'lm is engaging the person in different discoveries, then this is expected to increase the khasyah, humbleness, humility, submission, and taqwa of the person in one's relationship with Allah ﷻ.

In this sense, the true I'lm acquired by a true a'lim is mentioned as[65]

وَمِنَ النَّاسِ وَالدَّوَابِّ وَالْأَنْعَامِ مُخْتَلِفٌ أَلْوَانُهُ كَذَلِكَ إِنَّمَا يَخْشَى اللَّهَ مِنْ عِبَادِهِ الْعُلَمَاءُ إِنَّ اللَّهَ عَزِيزٌ غَفُورٌ {فاطر/28}.

One can possibly realize in this ayah everyone's journey as a being in this discovery of Names and Attributes of Allah ﷻ is different depending on their degrees of freedom وَمِنَ النَّاسِ وَالدَّوَابِّ وَالْأَنْعَامِ مُخْتَلِفٌ أَلْوَانُهُ.

Yet, the enhanced discoveries as given to humans with the Fadl of Allah ﷻ as mentioned وَعَلَّمَ آدَمَ الْأَسْمَاءَ كُلَّهَا require embodiment of khasyah of Allah ﷻ in this discovery and knowledge as mentioned إِنَّمَا يَخْشَى اللَّهَ مِنْ عِبَادِهِ الْعُلَمَاءُ. The lead embodiment of the true discoveries with ilm, khasyah, and taqwa is Rasulullah ﷺ.

Any knowledge or I'lm discovery with the absence of khasyah of Allah ﷻ can be self-destructive poison honey due to arrogance. The lead example of this Shaytān.

May Allah ﷻ protect us from following the path of Shaytān and make us follow of the path of Rasulullah ﷺ, Amìn. Allah ﷻ is beyond from all the similarities and examples, SubhanAllah!

Life and Existence Visibility and Reflection Names and Attributes of Allah ﷻ

Allah ﷻ is beyond from all the similarities and examples, SubhanAllah!

One should know that life or existence is similar to sunlight in visibility of the objects. The reflected light from the objects, make the object visible. Similarly, life and existence for a being is the light that make person realize the other beings.

Yet, at another level, both the observer and observed as a being is the reflection of the Primary Independent Light, al-Nûr, Allah ﷻ.

---

65. And among people and moving creatures and grazing livestock are various colors similarly. Only those fear Allah, from among His servants, who have knowledge. Indeed, Allah is Exalted in Might and Forgiving.

Yet, both the observer and observed as a being of life and existence is the reflection of the Primary Independent Life, al-Hayy, Allah ﷻ.

Yet, both the observer and observed as a being with life and existence reflects different Names and Attributes of Allah ﷻ.

One can call possibly state that the real discovery or visibility or seeing (basar) occurs with the reflection of the Names and Attributes of Allah ﷻ on the person and on these beings.

We are in existence and in life with the reflection of the Name and Attribute of Allah ﷻ as al-Hayy.

Allah ﷻ is beyond from all the similarities and examples, SubhanAllah!

Allah ﷻ is the Absolute Light, al-Nûr for the existence and life for all beings as mentioned اللَّهُ نُورُ السَّمَاوَاتِ وَالْأَرْضِ in Sûrah Nur in ayah 35. Allah ﷻ is beyond from all the similarities and examples, SubhanAllah!

As our existence and life is fully dependent on the One Who is Independent, al-Samad, our life and existence is the reflection of the Independent Nûr, Allah ﷻ.

With this reflected Nur of Allah ﷻ on us with life and existence, then we have a light that can see other beings with life and existence who also have the reflection of the Nur of Allah ﷻ with their existence and life.

In each being, we see different Names and Attributes of Allah ﷻ reflected on them in detail.

As one can see light has spectrum of different colorful lights, similarly some of the Names and Attributes of Allah ﷻ reflected on humans have this primary and inclusive required featured referred in terminology as Ismul-Ãzam. It is possible that there were salaf, who therefore thought al-Hayy is one of the Names and Attributes among Ismul-Ãzam. Allah ﷻ is beyond from all the similarities and examples, SubhanAllah!

As we talk about and try to approximate our limited human analogies with the Divine Transcendent Reality Allah ﷻ, one should embody constant adab in transgression of words, mind, or emotional wanderings.

Allah ﷻ is beyond from all the similarities and examples, SubhanAllah!

May Allah ﷻ forgive us, give me and us adab in our relationship with Allah ﷻ, Amìn.

Continuity of Existence

One should realize that we can continue to exist in this life and afterlife with the reflection of the Name and Attribute of Allah ﷻ as al-Qayyum after being created, brought into existence and in life by Allah ﷻ.

Allah ﷻ is the Owner of all dominions, Lahul mulk. Allah ﷻ can do whatever Allah ﷻ wills.

Continuity of existence is all from the Fadl, Rahmah and Grace of Allah ﷻ.

One should realize that the expression وَكُنتُمْ أَمْوَاتاً فَأَحْيَاكُمْ ثُمَّ يُمِيتُكُمْ ثُمَّ يُحْيِيكُمْ ثُمَّ إِلَيْهِ تُرْجَعُونَ can indicate the continuity of existence.

Yes, after the biggest ni'mah of existence, the second biggest ni'mah is the continuity of existence. Allah ﷻ could have terminated humans and Jinn after their life in this world. Allah ﷻ could have terminated humans and Jinn after their temporary life in afterlife.

Yet, due to the Divine Fadl, Karam, Grace, Rahmah, Allah ﷻ reflects another Divine Attribute and Name as al-Qayyum at a very shadow and minute scale on humans. Humans are not terminated or extinct as kuffar claim in the Qurān but continue their life once they are in the realm of existence. This is mentioned[66] أَيَعِدُكُمْ أَنَّكُمْ إِذَا مِتُّمْ وَكُنتُمْ تُرَابًا وَعِظَامًا أَنَّكُم مُّخْرَجُونَ {المؤمنون/35} هَيْهَاتَ هَيْهَاتَ لِمَا تُوعَدُونَ {المؤمنون/36} إِنْ هِيَ إِلَّا حَيَاتُنَا الدُّنْيَا نَمُوتُ وَنَحْيَا وَمَا نَحْنُ بِمَبْعُوثِينَ {المؤمنون/37}

These given initial privileges of Allah ﷻ to humans and Jinn with life, existence and continuity of existence are not taken from them due to the Grace, Fadl, Rahmah, and Karam of Allah ﷻ.

Even kuffar and kafir regardless of their position with Allah ﷻ are given life in this life and continue to exist in the afterlife with the Grace, Fadl, Rahmah, and Karam of Allah ﷻ.

SubhanAllah, Radina Billahi Rabba wa bil Islami Dina, wa bi Muhammadan Rasulan wa Nabiyya!

One should visit at this point the current and popular blur and artificial notions of Karma indicating reincarnation. This philosophical idea is sourced to be in some of the beliefs of Eastern religions such as Buddhism, Hinduism and even some pagan religions or traditions. Yet, this trend seemed to affect the people running away from the altered/

---

66. Does he promise you that when you have died and become dust and bones that you will be brought forth [once more]? How far, how far, is that which you are promised. Life is not but our worldly life - we die and live, but we will not be resurrected.

true theologies such as Judaism and made some of the followers so volatile in their strong clear instructions in their belief about afterlife.

One should remember that the ideas of karma and reincarnation are another sign of humans need showing their efforts of investigating and philosophizing this need through different discourses. The thirst for this need is there. The thirst for this need make people to seek, and interpret. Yet, they interpret without any data and proof. The interpretation is called speculation.

Yet, since this is an unknown reality and similar to throwing a rock to the sea of unseen, unknowns and invisible, then all these philosophies do not have any value unless there is a confirmation from the realities of unknowns that humans' philosophizing ideas about karma and reincarnation exist.

At its conceptual level, karma and reincarnation indicates a notion of accountability which is in line with the reality as instructed by Allah ﷻ.

Yet, as it happens a lot in human epistemology of knowledge, humans don't know where to draw lines in the interactions between limited human world of realities and the Infinite Transcendent Reality, Allah ﷻ.

The problem of trinity is due to basic epistemological or methodological error as a primary example. How can one or all humans let's say something or a knowledge about Allah ﷻ, the Infinite without any confirmation receiving this knowledge clearly and explicitly from Allah ﷻ? That is absurd, and methodologically illogical.

So, we really don't want to go to into endless discussions of trinity here if it makes sense or not but we are asking a very basic question, how can a teaching can be justified or canonized about the Transcendent, Infinite, Reality, Dhat of Allah ﷻ without getting confirmation from the Source, Allah ﷻ? Trinity has a problem and hole in its basic epistemological logical deduction.

The scriptures such as Torah, Bible, Gospel or the Qurān are the sources of confirmation of Allah ﷻ relating the Divine Dhat, Reality to humans. The question is then, is there anything explicit to emphasize this reality in any of these Divine Communications? The answers is no. Even the answer is opposite. Both Jewish and Muslim scholars are in agreement that Allah ﷻ mentions in the Qurān and Torah that Allah ﷻ is One, Unique and Infinite. All human attributes are antimorphic.

The Qurān strongly mentions in Sûrah ikhlas and in all different Sûrahs explicitly and repeatedly but Not implicitly about the Real Dhat of Allah ﷻ. The Quran explicitly and repeatedly indicates the fallacy of trinity as a naïve or purposeful/intentional speculation.

Methodology about the Unknown Realities

One should know that one of the main teachings of the Qurān and sunnah of Rasulullah ﷺ is that to establish a methodology about the realities of unseen, and unknown due to time such as about the past as mentioned[67] ذَلِكَ مِنْ أَنبَاءِ الْغَيْبِ نُوحِيهِ إِلَيكَ وَمَا كُنتَ لَدَيْهِمْ إِذْ يُلْقُون أَقْلَامَهُمْ أَيُّهُمْ يَكْفُلُ مَرْيَمَ وَمَا كُنتَ لَدَيْهِمْ إِذْ يَخْتَصِمُونَ {آل عمران/44}

The Qurān also establishes a methodology about other unknowns such as future predictions or unknowns due to lack of information about the life after death as mentioned[68] وَكَمْ أَهْلَكْنَا قَبْلَهُم مِّن قَرْنٍ هَلْ تُحِسُّ مِنْهُم مِّنْ أَحَدٍ أَوْ تَسْمَعُ لَهُمْ رِكْزًا {مريم/98}

The Qurān also establishes a methodology about other unknowns such due to lack of information due to the human limitations of knowing truly such as angels and true reality and knowledge about Allah ﷻ as mentioned[69] فَاسْتَفْتِهِمْ أَلِرَبِّكَ الْبَنَاتُ وَلَهُمُ الْبَنُونَ {الصافات/149} أَمْ خَلَقْنَا الْمَلَائِكَةَ إِنَاثًا وَهُمْ شَاهِدُونَ {الصافات/150} أَلَا إِنَّهُم مِّنْ إِفْكِهِمْ لَيَقُولُونَ {الصافات/151} وَلَدَ اللَّهُ وَإِنَّهُمْ لَكَاذِبُونَ {الصافات/152}[70] أَصْطَفَى الْبَنَاتِ عَلَى الْبَنِينَ مَا لَكُمْ كَيْفَ تَحْكُمُونَ {الصافات/154} أَفَلَا تَذَكَّرُونَ {الصافات/155} أَمْ لَكُمْ سُلْطَانٌ مُّبِينٌ {الصافات/156} فَأْتُوا بِكِتَابِكُمْ إِن كُنتُمْ صَادِقِينَ {الصافات/157} وَجَعَلُوا بَيْنَهُ وَبَيْنَ الْجِنَّةِ نَسَبًا وَلَقَدْ عَلِمَتِ الْجِنَّةُ إِنَّهُمْ لَمُحْضَرُونَ {الصافات/158} سُبْحَانَ اللَّهِ عَمَّا يَصِفُونَ {الصافات/159} إِلَّا عِبَادَ اللَّهِ الْمُخْلَصِينَ {الصافات/160}

---

67. That is from the news of the unseen which We reveal to you, [O Muhammad]. And you were not with them when they cast their pens as to which of them should be responsible for Mary. Nor were you with them when they disputed.

68. And how many have We destroyed before them of generations? Do you perceive of them anyone or hear from them a sound?

69. So inquire of them, [O Muhammad], "Does your Lord have daughters while they have sons?

70. Or did We create the angels as females while they were witnesses?" Unquestionably, it is out of their [invented] falsehood that they say, " Allah has begotten," and indeed, they are liars. Has He chosen daughters over sons? What is [wrong] with you? How do you make judgement? Then will you not be reminded? Or do you have a clear authority? Then produce your scripture, if you should be truthful. And they have claimed between Him and the jinn a lineage, but the jinn have already known that they [who made such claims] will be brought to [punishment]. Exalted is Allah above what they describe, Except the chosen servants of Allah [who do not share in that sin].

If we realize the above ayahs, there are very logical points that are underlined.

1. {الصافات/150} وَهُمْ شَاهِدُونَ: Allah ﷻ asks them if they have witness for their speculations or claims about the unknowns such as angels. The answer is no.

2. Allah ﷻ: كَيْفَ تَحْكُمُونَ {الصافات/154} أَفَلَا تَذَكَّرُونَ {الصافات/155} mentions to critically think in judgment calls and but not making speculative results. Results should follow critical thinking and logical premises and proofs. The answer is no.

3. {الصافات/156} أَمْ لَكُمْ سُلْطَانٌ مُبِينٌ: Logical results are based on clear data and proofs. How can a person base a result without any proof? The answer is no.

4. {الصافات/157} فَأْتُوا بِكِتَابِكُمْ إِنْ كُنْتُمْ صَادِقِينَ: Allah ﷻ sends scriptures with a knowledge about the unseen realities. Do they have another book that is sent by Allah ﷻ or any deity that is giving clear instructions about the unknown and unseen realities? Or they are some human speculations written or verbalized? The answer is no.

5. {الصافات/159} سُبْحَانَ اللَّهِ عَمَّا يَصِفُونَ: In all of these engagements for everyone, the critical expression of removal these diseases from the heart is "SubhanAllah." Yes, this dhikr and tasbih is so critical as Muslims we also get under the influence of these ideas. We need to remove them constantly from ourselves.

In this regard, humans get excited about especially speculations in future events. Even, Jinn help and misguide humans in these humans in vain efforts of speculations with all most all the time missing the realities.

Another case is the time of the End of Day. This is mentioned in the Qurān as[71] وَقَالَ الَّذِينَ كَفَرُوا لَا تَأْتِينَا السَّاعَةُ قُلْ بَلَى وَرَبِّي لَتَأْتِيَنَّكُمْ عَالِمِ الْغَيْبِ لَا يَعْزُبُ عَنْهُ مِثْقَالُ ذَرَّةٍ فِي السَّمَاوَاتِ وَلَا فِي الْأَرْضِ وَلَا أَصْغَرُ مِنْ ذَلِكَ وَلَا أَكْبَرُ إِلَّا فِي كِتَابٍ مُبِينٍ {سبأ/3}

---

71. But those who disbelieve say, "The Hour will not come to us." Say, "Yes, by my Lord, it will surely come to you. [Allah is] the Knower of the unseen." Not absent from Him is an atom's weight within the heavens or within the earth or [what is] smaller than that or greater, except that it is in a clear register -

The major part in human epistemology of knowledge, humans don't know where to draw lines in the interactions between limited human world of realities and the unseen world of afterlife, angels, and others.

How can reincarnation or karma can be justified if there is no confirmation of this idea from the unknown realities? They are all speculations unless clearly and explicitly mentioned in the scriptures such as the Qurān, Torah, Gospel or Bible about these Unknown realities as al-Gayb by the Infinite Transcendent Reality, Allah ﷻ.

One should remember that after having the true belief of tawhid, Oneness and Uniqueness of Allah ﷻ. The next required step in Islām, as the last updated, perfect and unchanged religion of Allah ﷻ until the End of Days, is the true belief in afterlife.

It is a wrong and very basic methodology to speculate about things that the person does not have clear proof, and knowledge. This is mentioned as[72] {النجم/35} أَعِندَهُ عِلْمُ الْغَيْبِ فَهُوَ يَرَى.

SubhanAllah, this ayah is exactly underlining today's scientific methodlogy!

The expression فَهُوَ يَرَى emphasize the correct methodology of experimentation, testing, confirming and triangulation. Yet, one cannot have this worldly methodology in the matter of al-ghayb because there is no confirmation as mentioned[73] وَكَمْ أَهْلَكْنَا قَبْلَهُم مِّن قَرْنٍ هَلْ تُحِسُّ مِنْهُم مِّنْ أَحَدٍ أَوْ تَسْمَعُ لَهُمْ رِكْزًا {مريم/98}.

As all the ayahs of the Qurān require sajdah, this ayah is another one that pushes the person on the ground to make sajdah, SubhanAllah! What does this ayah say or tell in its literal meaning and its broader meaning about the methodology of knowledge?

The ayah mentions that a lot of people died, destroyed or passed away before your generation. Do you hear even a sound (a click) from them? Then, how can you base your methodology afterlife or after death, if you really don't have any proof from the ones?

May Allah ﷻ make keep us on the path of the Qurān and Sunnah of Rasulullah ﷺ.

The person should follow at least a logic confirmed by a given knowledge about the unknown or al-ghayb by the Knower, Establisher

---

72. Does he have knowledge of the unseen, so he sees?
73. And how many have We destroyed before them of generations? Do you perceive of them anyone or hear from them a sound?

of al-ghaby, Alimul Ghayb, Allah ﷻ as mentioned[74] هُوَ أَلله الَّذِي لَا إِلَهَ إِلَّا هُوَ

عَالِمُ الْغَيْبِ وَالشَّهَادَةِ هُوَ الرَّحْمَنُ الرَّحِيمُ {الحشر/22}

This unknown knowledge is given in the Qurān and by Rasulullah
ﷺ. Therefore, all the beneficial guidelines for the knowledge of
unknowns/al-ghayb are sourced truly and authenticated by the Qurān
and delivered fully with the messengers and Sunnah of Rasulullah ﷺ as
mentioned[75] وَمَا هُوَ عَلَى الْغَيْبِ بِضَنِينٍ {التكوير/24}.

Speculations: Reincarnation & Karma

سَيَقُولُونَ ثَلَاثَةٌ رَّابِعُهُمْ كَلْبُهُمْ وَيَقُولُونَ خَمْسَةٌ سَادِسُهُمْ كَلْبُهُمْ رَجْمًا بِالْغَيْبِ وَيَقُولُونَ
سَبْعَةٌ وَثَامِنُهُمْ كَلْبُهُمْ قُل رَّبِّي أَعْلَمُ بِعِدَّتِهِم مَّا يَعْلَمُهُمْ إِلَّا قَلِيلٌ فَلَا تُمَارِ فِيهِمْ إِلَّا مِرَاء
ظَاهِرًا وَلَا تَسْتَفْتِ فِيهِم مِّنْهُمْ أَحَدًا {الكهف/22}[76]

وَقَدْ كَفَرُوا بِهِ مِن قَبْلُ وَيَقْذِفُونَ بِالْغَيْبِ مِن مَّكَانٍ بَعِيدٍ {سبأ/53}[77]

One should remember that Allah ﷻ hits the core of the today's and all
the times of speculations about al-gayb with the expression رَجْمًا بِالْغَيْبِ.

SubhanAllah!, Two words of the Qurān as رَجْمًا بِالْغَيْبِ hits and
destroys all the speculatively philosophized logics of reincarnation and
Karma.

This is the Ijaz of the Qurān! It is not the fourteen ayahs of the
Qurān that require sajdah but all the ayahs and expressions, words and
even letters of the Qurān require sajdatul tilawah!

The expression رَجْمًا بِالْغَيْبِ requires sajdatul tilawah for Allah ﷻ.

Two word expression destroys the plausibility thousands of books
written on this concept of reincarnation and Karma.

If we literally translate the expression رَجْمًا بِالْغَيْبِ, it is "throwing (a
stone) to the unknown (unseen). Here stone is mahzuf, hidden. Yet, the
word rajm can indicate throwing. The first thing that comes to mind in
Arabic language that goes with this word is stone.

---

74. He is Allah, other than whom there is no deity, Knower of the unseen and the witnessed.
He is the Entirely Merciful, the Especially Merciful.
75. And Muhammad is not a withholder of [knowledge of] the unseen.
76. None knows them except a few. So do not argue about them except with an obvious
argument, and do not inquire about them among [the speculators] from anyone
77. And they had already disbelieved in it before and would assault the unseen from a place
far away.

Yet, since it is mahzuf, it can especially indicate the speculations or ideas one throws or interprets similar to a stone with hits and misses.

If analyze this expression رَجْمًا بِالْغَيْبِ inside this ayah, Allah ﷻ exactly mentions this speculative approach of humans about something unknown as سَيَقُولُونَ ثَلَاثَةٌ رَّابِعُهُمْ كَلْبُهُمْ وَيَقُولُونَ خَمْسَةٌ سَادِسُهُمْ رَجْمًا بِالْغَيْبِ وَيَقُولُونَ سَبْعَةٌ وَثَامِنُهُمْ كَلْبُهُمْ قُل رَّبِّي أَعْلَمُ بِعِدَّتِهِم مَّا يَعْلَمُهُمْ إِلَّا قَلِيلٌ فَلَا تُمَارِ فِيهِمْ إِلَّا مِرَاء ظَاهِرًا وَلَا تَسْتَفْتِ فِيهِم مِّنْهُمْ أَحَدًا {الكهف/22}78.

The notion of speculation is some much emphasized that the ayah uses the style of itnab in the ijāz of the Qurān, a long descriptive style as:

▸ سَيَقُولُونَ: humans just speculate and will continue to speculate about things that they don't know. Here the letter س can indicate this humans' attitudes of speculations with the mudari/present form of continuity and future. The verb يَقُولُونَ indicate that is just a verbal demagogy, speculation and ungrounded interpretation.

▸ ثَلَاثَةٌ رَّابِعُهُمْ كَلْبُهُمْ: humans will try to speculate with numbers trying use some statistical arguments to justify these speculations.

▸ وَيَقُولُونَ خَمْسَةٌ سَادِسُهُمْ كَلْبُهُمْ: humans will continue to specucalte with numbers, statistical arguments and even changing prior stances to sound more scientific. One can remember the popular terms in new advances in science, science updates itself. It is funny that the planet Pluto was considered as a planet in all the science until few years ago. Then, they found that Pluto was a dwarf (planet).

▸ رَجْمًا بِالْغَيْبِ: In the middle of the ayah as a central or pivotal concept reminding the humans that there is a methodological error. If there are no proofs or any confirmation from these people or Allah ﷻ as Knower of all-Ghayb, all are speculations. They are as if throwing stone in the sea or space of unknowns.

▸ وَيَقُولُونَ سَبْعَةٌ وَثَامِنُهُمْ كَلْبُهُمْ: Humans will still continue speculate. Allah ﷻ mentions that humans run behind speculations

---

78. They will say there were three, the fourth of them being their dog; and they will say there were five, the sixth of them being their dog - guessing at the unseen; and they will say there were seven, and the eighth of them was their dog. Say, [O Muhammad], "My Lord is most knowing of their number. None knows them except a few. So do not argue about them except with an obvious argument and do not inquire about them among [the speculators] from anyone."

leaving the realities, clear and obvious signs. Even though the numbers of Ashab-I Kahf may be irrelevant or not important compared to speculations about Allah ﷻ and afterlife such as the speculations of reincarnation and karma, yet this repetition of the numbers for Ashab-Kahf members underlines very basic human error of renderings of speculations without any clear proof. At this point of the ayah, although some of the scholars think that this can be their real numbers of the Ashab-I Kahf because Allah ﷻ did not deny, yet, in the hit or miss concept of "throwing stone" to the unknown sea or space, even the person hits the reality, yet, one should not follow this approach of hit and miss in the very critical notions of imān to Allah ﷻ and afterlife. A guidance with the Qurān and the sunnah should be there as a triangulation method. In this case, Aristotle had a logical derivation of Oneness of Allah ﷻ in his book called metaphyiscs. Yet, true full and absolute knowledge of requires confirmation of this reality and all the realities with the true scriptures according to how Allah ﷻ relates the Divine Self. This is called triangulation of the current scientific method.

▶ رَّبِّي أَعْلَمُ بِعِدَّتِهِم مَّا يَعْلَمُهُمْ إِلَّا قَلِيلٌ: This part of the ayah establishes this true methodology of referring Gayb is known onnly by Allah ﷻ with all and true details and reality. Although there is a hit or miss as mentioned مَّا يَعْلَمُهُمْ إِلَّا قَلِيلٌ, one should follow the true guidelines as established by Allah ﷻ.

Another very clear and explicit ayah of humans' speculative approach about similar to throwing a rock or ideas without any proof is the ayah as[79] وَقَدْ كَفَرُوا بِهِ مِن قَبْلُ وَيَقْذِفُونَ بِالْغَيْبِ مِن مَّكَانٍ بَعِيدٍ {سبأ/53}.

In this ayah, Allah ﷻ emphasizes their speculative approach with وَيَقْذِفُونَ بِالْغَيْبِ as well as with the expression of مِن مَّكَانٍ بَعِيدٍ. The expression مِن مَّكَانٍ بَعِيدٍ addresses this basic problematic approach of speculation without any basis, clear foundation and simple methodology. Yet, there are a lot humans and Jinn that they are dragged behind these speculations wasting their life and afterlife.

May Allah ﷻ protect us, Amìn.

---

79. And they had already disbelieved in it before and would assault the unseen from a place far away.

Reality of Groups and Continuity of Life

One can ask if Allah ﷻ does not terminate the life of kuffar and kafir in the afterlife due to their oppression, zulm, then what is the purpose of continuity of life for them?

As we talk about groups, associations, and Jam'ah, after the individual make a choice with their free will a choice, then they spend their lives with the people who make the similar choice with them.

Kufr and nifāq attracts the people of kufr and nifāq to form a Jam'ah, group or association.

Imān attracts the people of imān to for a Jam'ah, group or association.

At a group or social level of existence, the hikmah and Divine Qadar Allah ﷻ requires to form these groups with a separation in this life and afterlife as mentioned[80]

قُلْ يَا أَيُّهَا الْكَافِرُونَ {الكافرون/1} لَا أَعْبُدُ مَا تَعْبُدُونَ {الكافرون/2} وَلَا أَنتُمْ عَابِدُونَ مَا أَعْبُدُ {الكافرون/3} وَلَا أَنَا عَابِدٌ مَّا عَبَدتُّمْ {الكافرون/4} وَلَا أَنتُمْ عَابِدُونَ مَا أَعْبُدُ {الكافرون/5} لَكُمْ دِينُكُمْ وَلِيَ دِينِ {الكافرون/6}

or

مَّا كَانَ اللَّهُ لِيَذَرَ الْمُؤْمِنِينَ عَلَى مَا أَنتُمْ عَلَيْهِ حَتَّىَ يَمِيزَ الْخَبِيثَ مِنَ الطَّيِّبِ وَمَا كَانَ اللَّهُ لِيُطْلِعَكُمْ عَلَى الْغَيْبِ وَلَكِنَّ اللَّهَ يَجْتَبِي مِن رُّسُلِهِ مَن يَشَاء فَآمِنُواْ بِاللَّهِ وَرُسُلِهِ وَإِن تُؤْمِنُواْ وَتَتَّقُواْ فَلَكُمْ أَجْرٌ عَظِيمٌ {آل عمران/179}[81]

In the above ayah mentioned with the word يَمِيزَ, or tamyiz and in others part of the Qurān, one of the hikmah is separation of groups and group associations. Although in this world, there can be a mix, yet, in the afterlife, a clear separation among groups will be there.

In this regard, kufr and nifāq bears a group, a place of group and a group leader. The place or house of the group is Jahannam. Their leader is Shaytān.

---

80. Say, "O disbelievers, I do not worship what you worship. Nor are you worshippers of what I worship. Nor will I be a worshipper of what you worship. Nor will you be worshippers of what I worship. For you is your religion, and for me is my religion."

81. Allah would not leave the believers in that [state] you are in [presently] until He separates the evil from the good. Nor would Allah reveal to you the unseen. But [instead], Allah chooses of His messengers whom He wills, so believe in Allah and His messengers. And if you believe and fear Him, then for you is a great reward.

Or, kufr requires the seed of Jahannam as a place of permanent abode with their Jam'ah, group and leader as Shayatìn as mentioned[82] وَسِيقَ الَّذِينَ كَفَرُوا إِلَى جَهَنَّمَ زُمَرًا حَتَّى إِذَا جَاؤُوهَا فُتِحَتْ أَبْوَابُهَا وَقَالَ لَهُمْ خَزَنَتُهَا أَلَمْ يَأْتِكُمْ رُسُلٌ مِّنكُمْ يَتْلُونَ عَلَيْكُمْ آيَاتِ رَبِّكُمْ وَيُنذِرُونَكُمْ لِقَاء يَوْمِكُمْ هَذَا قَالُوا بَلَى وَلَكِنْ حَقَّتْ كَلِمَةُ الْعَذَابِ عَلَى الْكَافِرِينَ {الزمر/71}

Similarly, imān requires a group, a place of group and a group leader. The place or house of the group is Jannah. The main leader is Rasulullah with other sub-leaders as other prophets.

Imān bears the seed of Jannah as a place of permanent abode with Jama'h, group and in the leadership of Rasulullah ﷺ, other Prophets. This is mentioned as[83] وَسِيقَ الَّذِينَ اتَّقَوْا رَبَّهُمْ إِلَى الْجَنَّةِ زُمَرًا حَتَّى إِذَا جَاؤُوهَا وَفُتِحَتْ أَبْوَابُهَا وَقَالَ لَهُمْ خَزَنَتُهَا سَلَامٌ عَلَيْكُمْ طِبْتُمْ فَادْخُلُوهَا خَالِدِينَ {الزمر/73}

The above Sûrah took the name of Zumar to indicate the reality of groups and group identiy in this life and afterlife. The ayahs especially indicate this group belonging identity with its continuity in this life and in afterlife.

Yet, Allah ﷻ and angels an all other beings are with the people of Imān due to their right and correct choice. In that sense, in the Jam'ah as indicated ahlullah or hizbullah Allah ﷻ and angels and all the people of imān can be present.

Allahumma Ja'alna min ahlullah, Amìn!

Yet, Allah ﷻ maintains the existence of current life due to the existence of people of imān still recognizing Allah ﷻ with a correct and real purpose and meaning. Therefore, Allah ﷻ sends blessings and showers them on earth as a whole. Both the kafir and mumin benefits from it. Yet, the source of real existence of these ni'mahs in this life is due to the people imān from Allah ﷻ as mentioned by Rasulullah ﷺ, al-Habib ﷺ.

---

82. And those who disbelieved will be driven to Hell in groups until, when they reach it, its gates are opened and its keepers will say, "Did there not come to you messengers from yourselves, reciting to you the verses of your Lord and warning you of the meeting of this Day of yours?" They will say, "Yes, but the word of punishment has come into effect upon the disbelievers.
83. But those who feared their Lord will be driven to Paradise in groups until, when they reach it while its gates have been opened and its keepers say, "Peace be upon you; you have become pure; so enter it to abide eternally therein," [they will enter].

Therefore, in the ayah of the Sûrah Hadid, kuffar try to seek the same benefit in the akhirah from the people of imān as mentioned[84] يَوْمَ يَقُولُ الْمُنَافِقُونَ وَالْمُنَافِقَاتُ لِلَّذِينَ آمَنُوا انظُرُونَا نَقْتَبِسْ مِن نُّورِكُمْ قِيلَ ارْجِعُوا وَرَاءكُمْ فَالْتَمِسُوا نُورًا فَضُرِبَ بَيْنَهُم بِسُورٍ لَّهُ بَابٌ بَاطِنُهُ فِيهِ الرَّحْمَةُ وَظَاهِرُهُ مِن قِبَلِهِ الْعَذَابُ {الحديد/13}.

Yet, now all the groups separate and there is no more a group such as people of imān benefitting the other group, people of kufr.

One should remember that people of Jahannam is still in n'imāh with existence, with continuation of life and they continue their life with their friends in afterlife. This still indicates Mercy, Rahmah and Adl-Justice of Allah ﷻ.

Why should one complain about their position in afterlife if they were happy with their friends in this life? They still continue with their true friendship in the akhirah.

Yet, true and intimate friendship of people of imān is with people of imān as mentioned in many places in the Qurān.

The true and intimate friendship of people of kufr is with people of kufr as mentioned in many places in the Qurān.

In akhirah, these true friendships are revealed, established, maintained, clarified and separated as mentioned[85] مَّا كَانَ اللّهُ لِيَذَرَ الْمُؤْمِنِينَ عَلَى مَا أَنتُمْ عَلَيْهِ حَتَّىَ يَمِيزَ الْخَبِيثَ مِنَ الطَّيِّبِ وَمَا كَانَ اللّهُ لِيُطْلِعَكُمْ عَلَى الْغَيْبِ وَلَكِنَّ اللّهَ يَجْتَبِي مِن رُّسُلِهِ مَن يَشَاء فَآمِنُواْ بِاللّهِ وَرُسُلِهِ وَإِن تُؤْمِنُواْ وَتَتَّقُواْ فَلَكُمْ أَجْرٌ عَظِيمٌ {آل عمران/179}

Reality of Imān

After all above discussions, one can now better understand the ayah[86] الم {البقرة/1} ذَلِكَ الْكِتَابُ لاَ رَيْبَ فِيهِ هُدًى لِّلْمُتَّقِينَ {البقرة/2} الَّذِينَ يُؤْمِنُونَ بِالْغَيْبِ وَيُقِيمُونَ الصَّلاةَ وَمِمَّا رَزَقْنَاهُمْ يُنفِقُونَ {البقرة/3}.

---

84. On the [same] Day the hypocrite men and hypocrite women will say to those who believed, "Wait for us that we may acquire some of your light." It will be said, "Go back behind you and seek light." And a wall will be placed between them with a door, its interior containing mercy, but on the outside of it is torment.
85. Allah would not leave the believers in that [state] you are in [presently] until He separates the evil from the good. Nor would Allah reveal to you the unseen. But [instead], Allah chooses of His messengers whom He wills, so believe in Allah and His messengers. And if you believe and fear Him, then for you is a great reward.
86. Alif, Lam, Meem. This is the Book about which there is no doubt, a guidance for those conscious of Allah - Who believe in the unseen, establish prayer, and spend out of what We have provided for them,

The real imān requires belief in al-ghayb. Yet, this belief in ghayb is outlined by the Qurān and Sunnah of Rasulullah ﷺ as mentioned الم {البقرة/1} ذَلِكَ الْكِتَابُ لاَ رَيْبَ فِيهِ.

Then this belief in ghayb referred as imān through the Qurān and sunnah of Rasulullah ﷺ is the guidance for the ones who embody them. They are called the people of taqwa as mentioned لِّلْمُتَّقِينَ.

The true embodiment of this imān is established with all the pillars of Islām such as Salāh, Zakāh as mentioned الصَّلاةَ وَمِمَّا رَزَقْنَاهُمْ يُنفِقُونَ.

The true imān requires belief in all the other scriptures sent by Allah ﷺ as mentioned وَالَّذِينَ يُؤْمِنُونَ بِمَا أُنزِلَ إِلَيْكَ وَمَا أُنزِلَ مِن قَبْلِكَ. Allah ﷺ did not leave people on earth without guidance.

Lastly, beyond the speculative approaches of al-ghayb such as afterlife with the popularized notions of reincarnation, karma or others, the ones who have taqwa confirm and belief in certainty about afterlife as outlined by the Qurān, Rasulullah ﷺ and other prophets as mentioned[87] وَبِالآخِرَةِ هُمْ يُوقِنُونَ {البقرة/4}.

These are the ones who are on guidance as mentioned أُوْلَئِكَ عَلَى هُدًى مِّن رَّبِّهِمْ compared to the ones who claim to be on guidance.

These are the ones who will be in the real happy and peaceful states of heart, mind and body in this life and afterlife as mentioned[88] وَأُوْلَئِكَ هُمُ الْمُفْلِحُونَ {البقرة/5}.

Allahumma Ja'alna min allazina siratul mustaqim
Siratallazina an'amta alayhim
Gayril m'agdubi alayhim wa la-dallìn,
Amìn.

Kufr & Shukr

When analyze the ayah[89] كَيْفَ تَكْفُرُونَ بِاللَّه وَكُنتُمْ أَمْوَاتاً فَأَحْيَاكُمْ ثُمَّ يُمِيتُكُمْ ثُمَّ يُحْيِيكُمْ ثُمَّ إِلَيْهِ تُرْجَعُونَ {البقرة/28} and all ayahs of the Qurān, one can realize the relationship between kufr and shukr.

It is fardh, wajib and required to thank and appreciate to the giver of a ni'mah.

---

87. And who believe in what has been revealed to you, [O Muhammad], and what was revealed before you, and of the Hereafter they are certain [in faith].
88. Those are upon [right] guidance from their Lord, and it is those who are the successful.
89. How can you disbelieve in Allah when you were lifeless and He brought you to life; then He will cause you to die, then He will bring you [back] to life, and then to Him you will be returned.

One should remember that thanking is not optional but required and wajib. Any person who gives us a ni'mah or benefit, it is required to thank to the giver of this ni'mah. This requirement is not and may not be clearly and explicitly mentioned in the classification of categorizations. Yet, if one thinks about it, it is logically harãm as well.

The whole notion of kufr in one's relationship with Allah ۞, kufr in one's relationship with parents, kufr in one's relationship of teachers, kufr in one's relationship of spouses and kufr in one's relationship of friends are all related.

If we really want to point out this critical notion, one think the opposite of kufr as shukr in the above relations with different categorizations as:

Shukr in One's Relationship With	Category
Allah SWT	Fardh
Parents	Wajib
Spouses, Teachers, & Friends that the person receive constant benefit/ni'mah	Sunnah-Muakkadah

The opposite of above table in the absence of shukr with the replacement of kufr would be:

Kufr in One's Relationship With	Category
Allah SWT	Harãm
Parents	Harãm
Spouses, Teachers, & Friends that the person receive constant benefit/ni'mah	Makrûh

In all above categorizations, one should realize that thanking, appreciating and showing gratitude is not optional but required for a Muslim.

In this regard, the form of thanking, appreciating, and showing gratitude can have different names as:

Form of Shukr in One's Relationship With	Category
Allah SWT	Ibadah
Parents	Nice Gentle Treatment/Fulfilling their needs/Taking care of them when they are old
Spouses, Teachers, & Friends that the person receive constant benefit/ni'mah	Nice Gentle Treatment/Fulfilling their needs

All above types and forms of shukr should be present naturally with eager and satisfaction of thanking. Yet, above all, one should make the main motivation to please Allah ﷻ. Especially, when a person does not have the natural embodiment of shukr as Rasulullah ﷺ did as he ﷺ mentioned "a fa lam takanu a'bdan shakurā," then the person should force him or herself to implement shukr to please Allah ﷻ. If that is not present there also, he or she implement with the fear of accountability and punishment in the akhirah for executing this harām shamelessly.

May Allah ﷻ protect us, Amìn.

[214]

أَمْ حَسِبْتُمْ أَن تَدْخُلُواْ الْجَنَّةَ وَلَمَّا يَأْتِكُم مَّثَلُ الَّذِينَ خَلَوْاْ مِن قَبْلِكُم مَّسَّتْهُمُ الْبَأْسَاءِ وَالضَّرَّاءِ وَزُلْزِلُواْ حَتَّى يَقُولَ الرَّسُولُ وَالَّذِينَ آمَنُواْ مَعَهُ مَتَى نَصْرُ اللّهِ أَلا إِنَّ نَصْرَ اللّهِ قَرِيبٌ
{البقرة/124}[90]

وَإِذَا أَذَقْنَا النَّاسَ رَحْمَةً مِّن بَعْدِ ضَرَّاءَ مَسَّتْهُمْ إِذَا لَهُم مَّكْرٌ فِي آيَاتِنَا قُلِ اللّهُ أَسْرَعُ مَكْرًا إِنَّ رُسُلَنَا يَكْتُبُونَ مَا تَمْكُرُونَ {يونس/21}[91]

---

90. Or do you think that you will enter Paradise while such [trial] has not yet come to you as came to those who passed on before you? They were touched by poverty and hardship and were shaken until [even their] messenger and those who believed with him said, "When is the help of Allah?" Unquestionably, the help of Allah is near.
91. And when We give the people a taste of mercy after adversity has touched them, at once they conspire against Our verses. Say, "Allah is swifter in strategy." Indeed, Our messengers record that which you conspire

وَلَئِنْ أَذَقْنَاهُ نَعْمَاءَ بَعْدَ ضَرَّاءَ مَسَّتْهُ لَيَقُولَنَّ ذَهَبَ السَّيِّئَاتُ عَنِّي إِنَّهُ لَفَرِحٌ فَخُورٌ {هود/10}[92]

وَلَئِنْ مَّسَّتْهُمْ نَفْحَةٌ مِّنْ عَذَابِ رَبِّكَ لَيَقُولُنَّ يَا وَيْلَنَا إِنَّا كُنَّا ظَالِمِينَ {الأنبياء/46}[93]

وَلَئِنْ أَذَقْنَاهُ رَحْمَةً مِّنَّا مِن بَعْدِ ضَرَّاء مَسَّتْهُ لَيَقُولَنَّ هَذَا لِي وَمَا أَظُنُّ السَّاعَةَ قَائِمَةً وَلَئِن رُّجِعْتُ إِلَى رَبِّي إِنَّ لِي عِندَهُ لَلْحُسْنَى فَلَنُنَبِّئَنَّ الَّذِينَ كَفَرُوا بِمَا عَمِلُوا وَلَنُذِيقَنَّهُم مِّنْ عَذَابٍ غَلِيظٍ {فصلت/50}[94]

Cycles of Difficulty-Easy

When we analyze the above ayahs with the common theme of مَّسَّتْهُمْ one should realize that Allah ﷻ is so Merciful that the trials tests and difficulties afflict us superficially.

The word مَّسَّتْ is and can be generally translated as "touch" to indicate the peripheral effects of these trials, tests and difficulties. Yet, humans are impatient and not tolerant handling any evil-looking incident or difficulty. We mostly scream out and complain a lot as if we were pressed down hard. May Allah ﷻ protect us and give us a'fiyah, Amin.

On the other hand, the nim'ah that we are constantly in is expressed with أَذَقْنَاهُ.

Again, it is the Mercy and Rahmah of Allah ﷻ that the difficulties or trials are peripheral and temporal as mentioned with مَّسَّتْهُمْ and the ni'mahs are continuous with constant envelopment expressed with أَذَقْنَاهُ.

Handling Cycles of Difficulties & Easy: People of Iman

Yet, this affliction how it is perceived and how noble or lowly can depend on the audience.

---

92. But if We give him a taste of favor after hardship has touched him, he will surely say, "Bad times have left me." Indeed, he is exultant and boastful -
93. And if [as much as] a whiff of the punishment of your Lord should touch them, they would surely say, "O woe to us! Indeed, we have been wrongdoers."
94. And if We let him taste mercy from Us after an adversity which has touched him, he will surely say, "This is [due] to me, and I do not think the Hour will occur; and [even] if I should be returned to my Lord, indeed, for me there will be with Him the best." But We will surely inform those who disbelieved about what they did, and We will surely make them taste a massive punishment.

For the people of imān struggling on the path of Allah ﷻ, the difficulties can be noble. This can be mentioned as[95] أَمْ حَسِبْتُمْ أَن تَدْخُلُواْ الْجَنَّةَ وَلَمَّا يَأْتِكُم مَّثَلُ الَّذِينَ خَلَوْاْ مِن قَبْلِكُم مَّسَّتْهُمُ الْبَأْسَاء وَالضَّرَّاء وَزُلْزِلُواْ حَتَّى يَقُولَ الرَّسُولُ وَالَّذِينَ آمَنُواْ مَعَهُ مَتَى نَصْرُ اللَّهِ أَلا إِنَّ نَصْرَ اللَّهِ قَرِيبٌ {البقرة/214}

In this regard, istiqamah on the path of Allah ﷻ requires to continue but not to stop due to being discouraged from handicaps, blocks, tests and trials on the journey.

For example, if a person trips and falls while walking, it is expected that a sound minded person would stand up and continue walking.

He can look and try to analyze the reasons why he tripped or if he did something wrong. He can observe the platform and talk to people around him about this accident.

Yet, one of the critical positions on the path of Allah ﷻ is istiqāmah to move on without making not much deal of the hindrances, blocks or barriers.

Yes, one can make an internal muhasabah-accountability why this incident happened. Yet, after immediately making istigfar and tawbah, the person still moves on the journey towards one's aimed vertical relation with Allah ﷻ.

Today's problem of theodicy, blaming God when something evil-looking happens in one's life is due to the lack of purpose, aim, and most importantly lack of istiqamah.

Istiqamah requires a goal-oriented approach.

Muhasabah requires a means-oriented approach.

Both the means and goals should be halal in usul-fiqh when a person is trying to do something to please Allah ﷻ.

In other words, a high long-term goal pleasing Allah ﷻ is only achieved with the high short-term struggle to please Allah ﷻ. Both means and ends should be halal and permissible by Allah ﷻ.

One should adapt both istiqamah and muhasabah on the path of Allah ﷻ to please Allah ﷻ.

There is always a balance and a middle way needed on the path.

---

95. Or do you think that you will enter Paradise while such [trial] has not yet come to you as came to those who passed on before you? They were touched by poverty and hardship and were shaken until [even their] messenger and those who believed with him said, "When is the help of Allah?" Unquestionably, the help of Allah is near.

When the person is discouraged on the path and get pessimistic, then he or she increase one's istiqamah-goal oriented related approach or attitude.

When the person is overjoyed with the achievements on the path of Allah ﷻ to please Allah ﷻ, then he or she can increase the muhasabah oriented related approach or attitude in front of Allah ﷻ, Rabbul Alamin.

The first case related with discouragement can lead to the spiritual states of kabz. If this state is not properly managed then, the person can become pessimistic, hopeless, and lazy in life and on the struggle of path of Allah ﷻ.

The second case related with overjoy can lead to the spiritual states of bast. If this state is not properly managed, then the person can lose ikhlas and can only be motivated with results. In this case, the pleasure of Allah ﷻ can be shadowed with external-looking poisonous achievements.

One should strive to achieve on the path of Allah ﷻ. As the achievements increase on the path, one should both increase one's muhasabah with istighfar and tawbah to Allah ﷻ and tanzih of Allah ﷻ, and at the same time, one should increase their hamd showing genuine gratitude and appreciation for the ni'mahs of Allah ﷻ. This is state and maqām is summarized in[96] إِذَا جَاءَ نَصْرُ أَللهِ وَالْفَتْحُ {النصر/1} وَرَأَيْتَ النَّاسَ يَدْخُلُونَ

فِي دِينِ اللَّهِ أَفْوَاجًا {النصر/2} فَسَبِّحْ بِحَمْدِ رَبِّكَ وَاسْتَغْفِرْهُ إِنَّهُ كَانَ تَوَّابًا {النصر/3}

The embodiment of this maqām is Rasulullah ﷺ, al-Habib ﷺ, the Owner of the Maqām of Mahmûd ﷺ.

Handling Cycles of Difficulties & Easy: People of Kufr and People with Mixed States of Imān

One can realize the attitudes of people of kufr when afflicted with an evil-looking incident and then, when Allah ﷻ removes their difficulty, they become and maintain the attitude of belligerence. This is mentioned as[97] وَإِذَا أَذَقْنَا النَّاسَ رَحْمَةً مِّن بَعْدِ ضَرَّاءَ مَسَّتْهُمْ إِذَا لَهُم مَّكْرٌ فِي آيَاتِنَا قُلِ أَللهُ أَسْرَعُ مَكْرًا إِنَّ

رُسُلَنَا يَكْتُبُونَ مَا تَمْكُرُونَ {يونس/21}

---

96. When the victory of Allah has come and the conquest, And you see the people entering into the religion of Allah in multitudes, Then exalt [Him] with praise of your Lord and ask forgiveness of Him. Indeed, He is ever Accepting of repentance.

97. And when We give the people a taste of mercy after adversity has touched them, at once they conspire against Our verses. Say, "Allah is swifter in strategy." Indeed, Our messengers record that which you conspire

As we analyze further the attitudes of people for the cycle of
difficulty and ease as given by Allah ﷻ, there can be people who may call
themselves believers, or people of imān, yet they may show some traits
or attitudes of kufr due to how they interpret this cycle of difficulty and
ease.

For example,[98] وَلَئِنْ أَذَقْنَاهُ نَعْمَاءَ بَعْدَ ضَرَّاءَ مَسَّتْهُ لَيَقُولَنَّ ذَهَبَ السَّيِّئَاتُ عَنِّي إِنَّهُ
لَفَرِحٌ فَخُورٌ {10/هود}

After the cycle of difficulty, the precedent circumstances of ease can
make these people wrongly interpret that the presence of easy is due to
the removal of their sins ذَهَبَ السَّيِّئَاتُ عَنِّي. Yet, no one is safe from their
ending in front of Allah ﷻ until they meet with Allah ﷻ with death.

Another category are the people who do not change their disposition
or life perspective or life style unless they are afflicted with something in
their life. This is mentioned as[99] وَلَئِنْ مَّسَّتْهُمْ نَفْحَةٌ مِّنْ عَذَابِ رَبِّكَ لَيَقُولُنَّ يَا وَيْلَنَا إِنَّا
كُنَّا ظَالِمِينَ {46/الأنبياء}

Yet, if this change is early in their life, then it can be possibly a good
change. If this change is made sometime late in their life, it may still be
good but it may have a lot of regrets for their prior life with oppression
and zulm. If this change is made right at the last minute before death,
Allah ﷻ knows if it is acceptable or if it is a good or a bad change. One
can remember the tawbah of Fir'awn in the last minute of his death. In
all the situations, Allah ﷻ is the ultimate Judge in one's relationship with
Allah ﷻ.

Another example is[100] وَلَئِنْ أَذَقْنَاهُ رَحْمَةً مِّنَّا مِن بَعْدِ ضَرَّاءَ مَسَّتْهُ لَيَقُولَنَّ هَذَا لِي
وَمَا أَظُنُّ السَّاعَةَ قَائِمَةً وَلَئِنْ رُجِعْتُ إِلَى رَبِّي إِنَّ لِي عِندَهُ لَلْحُسْنَى فَلَنُنَبِّئَنَّ الَّذِينَ كَفَرُوا بِمَا
عَمِلُوا وَلَنُذِيقَنَّهُم مِّنْ عَذَابٍ غَلِيظٍ {50/فصلت}

These types of people can have some wrong expectations from
Rabbul Alamìn that are not in line with the Qurān and sunnah of
Rasulullah ﷺ.

---

98. But if We give him a taste of favor after hardship has touched him, he will surely say, "Bad
times have left me." Indeed, he is exultant and boastful -
99. And if [as much as] a whiff of the punishment of your Lord should touch them, they would
surely say, "O woe to us! Indeed, we have been wrongdoers."
100. And if We let him taste mercy from Us after an adversity which has touched him, he will
surely say, "This is [due] to me, and I do not think the Hour will occur; and [even] if I should be
returned to my Lord, indeed, for me there will be with Him the best." But We will surely inform
those who disbelieved about what they did, and We will surely make them taste a massive
punishment.

For example, a person of imān cannot claim وَمَا أَظُنُّ السَّاعَةَ قَائِمَةً and yet at the same time believe وَلَئِن رُّجِعْتُ إِلَى رَبِّي إِنَّ لِي عِندَهُ لَلْحُسْنَى. This is a typical approach among ahlu-kitāb to adapt a pick and choose method of following the religion.

Yet, religion, dîn of Allah ﷻ is complementary, perfect and harmonious. One belief complements the other.

Therefore, in the Islamic usûl of creed system, if a person believes part of the religion and does not believe the other part, then he or she is considered at the out fold of Islām. The reason for that is the teachings of Allah ﷻ is complementary, perfect and harmonious as implemented by Rasulullah ﷺ. This is especially critical in the belief/creed system of Islām.

In the applications, there may be some differences as allowed by Rasulullah ﷺ, sahabah, tabi'un and salaf to acknowledge changing times, culture, context and people with different backgrounds. The acceptance of these differences in the applications can be another sign for the Mercy and Rahmah of Allah ﷻ for us.

Allahumma Ja'alna attibu' sunnata Rasulullah ﷺ, Muhammad ﷺ, Amìn.

Juz 4

Sûrah 3 Āl-Ìmrān

[191]

الَّذِينَ يَذْكُرُونَ اللهَ قِيَامًا وَقُعُودًا وَعَلَىٰ جُنُوبِهِمْ وَيَتَفَكَّرُونَ فِي خَلْقِ السَّمَاوَاتِ وَالْأَرْضِ رَبَّنَا مَا خَلَقْتَ هَذَا بَاطِلاً سُبْحَانَكَ فَقِنَا عَذَابَ النَّارِ {آل عمران/191}[101]

The Real Critical Thinking

It is important to realize that Allah ﷻ encourages critical thinking constantly as mentioned with وَيَتَفَكَّرُونَ فِي خَلْقِ السَّمَاوَاتِ وَالْأَرْضِ. This critical thinking can be also called science as popularized today in the

---

101. Who remember Allah while standing or sitting or [lying] on their sides and give thought to the creation of the heavens and the earth, [saying], "Our Lord, You did not create this aimlessly; exalted are You [above such a thing]; then protect us from the punishment of the Fire.

incidents, discoveries and inventions through nature, galaxies, and other means of experimentation in the realities of our existence.

Yet, the real reality of critical thinking should lead to true amazements through imān, dhikr and remembrance of Allah ﷻ constantly in all physical and spiritual positions of standing, sitting and lying down as mentioned الَّذِينَ يَذْكُرُونَ اللّٰهَ قِيَامًا وَقُعُودًا وَعَلَىٰ جُنُوبِهِمْ. This critical thinking then becomes a true, real and purposeful critical thinking. SubhanAllah!

Statistical Impossibility Trends in Science

When a person of science or scientific knowledge is amazed with science, if he or she does not take the required, natural and fitri state of imān, purpose, and meaning for these complex and complicated structures under the origination and maintenance of Rabbul Alamin, then some , especially today, tend to run behind the impossible statistical arguments. These impossible statistical arguments assume and claim their foundational premises on purposelessness, randomness, and disorder.

Yet, this promise or assumption itself is faulty due to the nature of the assumed entity. In other words, the scientists find, observe, and try to understand the nature with its complex and ordered structure. They find nature in a super structured system and order but yet, some of them claim and interpret this complex order with aimless, randomness and with impossible statistical arguments.

This logic itself is faulty. In the realities of causality, there is a causal relationship. An order leads to an ordered structure. For example, when a person is building a house. There is first a bare land. Then, external pillars are built by the constructors. Then, the base, sidewalls, roof and plumbing, electric work, heating ducts. Then, painting, flooring, doors, door knobs, windows, appliances and other parts are installed. Yet, this simple house goes through the steps of order, structure, expertise, and causality. Any type of disorder between the sequences, or during the process such as a fire accident can demolish all the established efforts.

Similarly, it is absurd, and illogical to assume a very complex and complicated structured system of this universe to come out from random, impossible statistical arguments, and chaos. SubhanAllah!

Purposelessness Trends in Science

Then, one can ask the builder as "What is the purpose of this house?"

He may say that "it is goal and purpose is for residence. If I don't have the purpose in the beginning, how can I know what I am going to build? I should have first the intention and purpose to build this house. I think and plan with the architects everything before. Then, action of building comes next."

Similarly, Allah ﷻ has originated, created, bestowed and given us this complex and complicated structured universe with a purpose as mentioned مَا خَلَقْتَ هَذَا بَاطِلاً. This purpose is to constantly increase one's imān through the levels of yaqìn certainty by applying the methodology of critical thinking وَيَتَفَكَّرُونَ فِي خَلْقِ السَّمَاوَاتِ وَالأَرْضِ.

Then, this leads to the natural and fitri states of remembrance of Allah ﷻ in all positions as mentioned الَّذِينَ يَذْكُرُونَ اللَّهَ قِيَامًا وَقُعُودًا وَعَلَى جُنُوبِهِمْ. This is the essence. This dhikr and remembrance of Allah ﷻ in its general form is called I'badah for the purpose of our existence and creation as mentioned[102] {الذاريات/56} وَمَا خَلَقْتُ الْجِنَّ وَالإِنْسَ إِلاَّ لِيَعْبُدُونِ

Yet, the essence of 'ibadah is dhikr, remembrance of Allah ﷻ at all times as mentioned[103] اتْلُ مَا أُوحِيَ إِلَيْكَ مِنَ الْكِتَابِ وَأَقِمِ الصَّلاَةَ إِنَّ الصَّلاَةَ تَنْهَى عَنِ الْفَحْشَاءِ وَالْمُنكَرِ وَلَذِكْرُ اللَّهِ أَكْبَرُ وَاللَّهُ يَعْلَمُ مَا تَصْنَعُونَ {العنكبوت/54}

When one reviews the ayah وَيَتَفَكَّرُونَ فِي خَلْقِ السَّمَاوَاتِ وَالأَرْضِ رَبَّنَا مَا خَلَقْتَ هَذَا بَاطِلاً, the expression مَا خَلَقْتَ هَذَا بَاطِلاً can nullify these impossible claims of statistical arguments existence and with its assumed claims of aimlessness or existence without purpose. SubhanAllah!

Purpose: 'Ibadah & Amal

When one reviews the purpose of humans in the Qurān and life of Rasulullah ﷺ, there is the 'ibadah and amal-u salih, good, moral and ethical actions and engagements. Yet, both require embodying the dhikr, remembrance of Allah ﷻ before, during and after these engagements.

Allah ﷻ mentions the amal/action perspective of our existence as[104] الَّذِي خَلَقَ الْمَوْتَ وَالْحَيَاةَ لِيَبْلُوَكُمْ أَيُّكُمْ أَحْسَنُ عَمَلاً وَهُوَ الْعَزِيزُ الْغَفُورُ {الملك/2}

---

102. And I did not create the jinn and mankind except to worship Me.
103. Recite, [O Muhammad], what has been revealed to you of the Book and establish prayer. Indeed, prayer prohibits immorality and wrongdoing, and the remembrance of Allah is greater. And Allah knows that which you do.
104. [He] who created death and life to test you [as to] which of you is best in deed - and He is the Exalted in Might, the Forgiving -

Allah ﷻ mentions the 'ibadah/worship perspective our existence as[105]
{الذاريات/56} وَمَا خَلَقْتُ الْجِنَّ وَالْإِنسَ إِلَّا لِيَعْبُدُونِ.

Yet, both require the true embodiment of remembrance of Allah ﷻ, Dhikrullah as mentioned اتْلُ مَا أُوحِيَ إِلَيْكَ مِنَ الْكِتَابِ وَأَقِمِ الصَّلَاةَ إِنَّ الصَّلَاةَ تَنْهَى عَنِ الْفَحْشَاءِ وَالْمُنكَرِ وَلَذِكْرُ اللَّهِ أَكْبَرُ وَاللَّهُ يَعْلَمُ مَا تَصْنَعُونَ {العنكبوت/45}

The expression وَلَذِكْرُ اللَّهِ أَكْبَرُ can indicate this true essence of 'ibadah and amal. One can call this essence as the rûh or soul of our 'ibadah and amal. This true essence is before the engagement of 'ibadah and amal as an intention and preparation, during the engagement of 'ibadah and amal as the embodiment of this engagement, after the engagement of 'ibadah and amal as the completion of this engagement with hamd/ gratitude and istighfār/asking forgiveness for any possible insincerity or lack of ikhlas.

The continuity of Dhikrullah in both 'ibadah and amal can lead to the maqām of ihsān and then, the person can be referred as from the muhsinìn as mentioned in hadith Jibril [2]. SubhanAllah!

Tanzih & Kufr

One should remember that engagements of partial and full incidents of attributing chance, chaos, randomness, statistical arguments, aimlessness and without purpose in all the creation beyond true tawhid with La ilaha illa Allah Muhammadun Rasulullah and beyond true purpose with the true essence of Dhikrullah in the embodiment of 'ibadah and amal require tanzih as mentioned in the ayah سُبْحَانَكَ.

Depending on the absence of this tanzih during any mental, emotional and physical engagement, the person can be deemed to deserve punishment due to not fulfilling the essence of their existence in life with this essence of true Dhikrullah in 'ibadah and amal as mentioned فَقِنَا عَذَابَ النَّارِ.

SubnahAllah wa bihamdihi astagfiruka wa attubu ilayk adada khalqik, wa rida nafsik wa zinata arshik,

May Allah ﷻ protect from the punishment of Jahannam with the Divine Fadl and Karam, Amìn.

---

105. And I did not create the jinn and mankind except to worship Me.

Juz 10

Sûrah 9 - al-Tawbah

[38-41]

يَا أَيُّهَا الَّذِينَ آمَنُواْ مَا لَكُمْ إِذَا قِيلَ لَكُمُ انفِرُواْ فِي سَبِيلِ اللّهِ اثَّاقَلْتُمْ إِلَى الأَرْضِ أَرَضِيتُم بِالْحَيَاةِ الدُّنْيَا مِنَ الآخِرَةِ فَمَا مَتَاعُ الْحَيَاةِ الدُّنْيَا فِي الآخِرَةِ إِلاَّ قَلِيلٌ {التوبة/38}106 إِلاَّ تَنفِرُواْ يُعَذِّبْكُمْ عَذَابًا أَلِيمًا وَيَسْتَبْدِلْ قَوْمًا غَيْرَكُمْ وَلاَ تَضُرُّوهُ شَيْئًا وَاللّهُ عَلَى كُلِّ شَيْءٍ قَدِيرٌ {التوبة/39} إِلاَّ تَنصُرُوهُ فَقَدْ نَصَرَهُ اللّهُ إِذْ أَخْرَجَهُ الَّذِينَ كَفَرُواْ ثَانِيَ اثْنَيْنِ إِذْ هُمَا فِي الْغَارِ إِذْ يَقُولُ لِصَاحِبِهِ لاَ تَحْزَنْ إِنَّ اللّهَ مَعَنَا فَأَنزَلَ اللّهُ سَكِينَتَهُ عَلَيْهِ وَأَيَّدَهُ بِجُنُودٍ لَّمْ تَرَوْهَا وَجَعَلَ كَلِمَةَ الَّذِينَ كَفَرُواْ السُّفْلَى وَكَلِمَةُ اللّهِ هِيَ الْعُلْيَا وَاللّهُ عَزِيزٌ حَكِيمٌ {التوبة/40} انفِرُواْ خِفَافًا وَثِقَالاً وَجَاهِدُواْ بِأَمْوَالِكُمْ وَأَنفُسِكُمْ فِي سَبِيلِ اللّهِ ذَلِكُمْ خَيْرٌ لَّكُمْ إِن كُنتُمْ تَعْلَمُونَ {التوبة/41}

Being Together For the Sake of Allah ﷻ

When we analyze the expression إِلاَّ تَنفِرُواْ يُعَذِّبْكُمْ عَذَابًا in the ayah أَلِيمًا وَيَسْتَبْدِلْ قَوْمًا غَيْرَكُمْ وَلاَ تَضُرُّوهُ شَيْئًا وَاللّهُ عَلَى كُلِّ شَيْءٍ قَدِيرٌ {التوبة/39}, one can realize the encouragement of the zeal for getting together to do good for the sake of Allah ﷻ. In that sense, a person should do the utmost effort to work together as a group, jam'ah, and collectively in the matters of social, and communal good. One can call these efforts as dawah, jihād, tablihg or amri bil ma'ruf wa nahyi anil munkar.

---

106. O you who have believed, what is [the matter] with you that, when you are told to go forth in the cause of Allah, you adhere heavily to the earth? Are you satisfied with the life of this world rather than the Hereafter? But what is the enjoyment of worldly life compared to the Hereafter except a [very] little. If you do not go forth, He will punish you with a painful punishment and will replace you with another people, and you will not harm Him at all. And Allah is over all things competent. If you do not aid the Prophet - Allah has already aided him when those who disbelieved had driven him out [of Makkah] as one of two, when they were in the cave and he said to his companion, "Do not grieve; indeed Allah is with us." And Allah sent down his tranquility upon him and supported him with angels you did not see and made the word of those who disbelieved the lowest, while the word of Allah - that is the highest. And Allah is Exalted in Might and Wise. Go forth, whether light or heavy, and strive with your wealth and your lives in the cause of Allah. That is better for you, if you only knew.

Helping the People who are trying to do good for the sake of Allah ﷻ

When we analyze the expression إلاَّ تَنصُرُوهُ فَقَدْ in the ayah[107] نَصَرَهُ اللّهُ إِذْ أَخْرَجَهُ الَّذِينَ كَفَرُواْ ثَانِيَ اثْنَيْنِ إِذْ هُمَا فِي الْغَارِ إِذْ يَقُولُ لِصَاحِبِهِ لاَ تَحْزَنْ إِنَّ اللّهَ مَعَنَا فَأَنزَلَ اللّهُ سَكِينَتَهُ عَلَيْهِ وَأَيَّدَهُ بِجُنُودٍ لَّمْ تَرَوْهَا وَجَعَلَ كَلِمَةَ الَّذِينَ كَفَرُواْ السُّفْلَى وَكَلِمَةُ اللّهِ هِيَ الْعُلْيَا وَاللّهُ عَزِيزٌ حَكِيمٌ {40/التوبة}[108], this can indicate the attitude of helping the people and supporting in the matters of the good for the sake of Allah ﷻ. The primary sabab-nuzul of this ayah Rasulullah ﷺ as the embodiment of the good to please Allah ﷻ. The warning or teaching is initially addressing the sahabah (ranhum).

Being Enthusiastic to Do Good for the Sake of Allah ﷻ

When we analyze the ayah[109] انْفِرُواْ خِفَافًا وَثِقَالاً وَجَاهِدُواْ بِأَمْوَالِكُمْ وَأَنفُسِكُمْ فِي سَبِيلِ اللّهِ ذَلِكُمْ خَيْرٌ لَّكُمْ إِن كُنتُمْ تَعْلَمُونَ {41/التوبة}, one can realize that Allah ﷻ indicate to have the attitude of participating in the works of the dìn with enthusiasm regardless of its size of our efforts. Sometimes, our negative attitudes discourage people. Yet, if we just join with the intention of "how I can help or how I can contribute for all the good things that you are doing", then this attitude can encourage others. The results of these good works can be multiplied with the multiple effects of good outcomes graced by Allah ﷻ.

Possibility of always Replacement Due to Change of Life Goals to Please Allah ﷻ

When we analyze the ayah[110] يَا أَيُّهَا الَّذِينَ آمَنُواْ مَا لَكُمْ إِذَا قِيلَ لَكُمُ انفِرُواْ فِي سَبِيلِ اللّهِ اثَّاقَلْتُمْ إِلَى الأَرْضِ أَرَضِيتُم بِالْحَيَاةِ الدُّنْيَا مِنَ الآخِرَةِ فَمَا مَتَاعُ الْحَيَاةِ الدُّنْيَا فِي الآخِرَةِ إِلاَّ قَلِيلٌ and إِلاَّ تَنفِرُواْ يُعَذِّبْكُمْ عَذَابًا أَلِيمًا وَيَسْتَبْدِلْ قَوْمًا غَيْرَكُمْ وَلاَ تَضُرُّوهُ شَيْئًا {38/التوبة}

---

107. If you do not aid the Prophet - Allah has already aided him when those who disbelieved had driven him out [of Makkah] as one of two, when they were in the cave and he said to his companion, "Do not grieve; indeed Allah is with us." And Allah sent down his tranquillity upon him and supported him with angels you did not see and made the word of those who disbelieved the lowest, while the word of Allah - that is the highest. And Allah is Exalted in Might and Wise.

108. Go forth, whether light or heavy, and strive with your wealth and your lives in the cause of Allah. That is better for you, if you only knew.

109. Go forth, whether light or heavy, and strive with your wealth and your lives in the cause of Allah. That is better for you, if you only knew.

110. O you who have believed, what is [the matter] with you that, when you are told to go forth in the cause of Allah, you adhere heavily to the earth? Are you satisfied with the life of this world rather than the Hereafter? But what is the enjoyment of worldly life compared to the Hereafter except a [very] little.

وَاللَّهُ عَلَى كُلِّ شَيْءٍ قَدِيرٌ {التوبة/39}¹¹¹, one of the main problems is the change of the goals and intentions for the sake of Allah ﷻ on the journey of pleasing Allah ﷻ.

When we analyze these ayahs, one can realize that people could have initially good intentions and motivation to please Allah ﷻ for a certain period of time. Yet, this initial virtuous intention and motivation can be replaced overtime and slowly with the lowly intentions and motivations of worldly gains instead of the initial high intentions of pleasing Allah ﷻ.

Therefore, no one has a guarantee and assurance that they will end journey of pleasing Allah ﷻ in the virtuous and noble way they initially have started this journey. One of the most tragic cases can be a person who were motivated to please Allah ﷻ, made hijrah, sacrificed so much physically and from their wealth, and then he or she spends last portions of their life span in acquiring wealth, disconnecting themselves in the works of dīn, and justifying what or why they are doing with an answer of "everyone is doing the same, therefore...."

One of the main diseases of the heart is the justification or normalizing a lowly or a bad trait due to the collective trends in the groups or societies. A person doing an evil because everyone is doing it. A person cheating because everyone is cheating in the society, jam'ah or institution. A person is a drug addict because everyone is doing it. A person disobeying the parents because everyone is doing it. A person not going to church or mosque because everyone is doing it. A person is a skeptic, atheist or not appreciating Allah ﷻ because everyone is doing it.

SubhanAllah! where is the popularized method of "critical thinking" in these engagements?

One of the worst cases of this normalization is that the concept of "If I don't do it, then I will be considered as stupid or outcast..." This is called as "being cool" in the informal language. For the sake of being cool, a lot of teenagers, college students and youth do a lot of evil things due to following their peers, groups, or exclusive or inclusive societies. Yet, adults can project the same idea of "being cool" similarly as "If I don't do it, then I will be considered as stupid..."

SubhanAllah! where is the popularized method of "critical thinking" in these blind submissions?

---

111. If you do not go forth, He will punish you with a painful punishment and will replace you with another people, and you will not harm Him at all. And Allah is over all things competent.

When collective body of people increase in a jam'ah or a group, not valuing the works and efforts done for the sake of Allah ﷻ, criticizing them, and even discouraging the people who wants to do some good work, then this means that there is spiritual disease that is deadlier than cancer in this person or among these individuals. Yet, physical or bodily cancer only kills the body in this short life. A spiritual cancer such as this one can ruin and kill one's entire infinite afterlife, May Allah ﷻ protect us from all the diseases of heart, mind and body, Amìn.

As it is the sunnatullah, as these spiritual cancers kills these individuals, groups or jam'ah, then Allah ﷻ originates, gives life to others and replaces the previous individuals, groups, or jam'ah as mentioned وَيَسْتَبْدِلْ قَوْمًا غَيْرَكُمْ.

One should remember that from the Qadar point of view, no one can blame Allah ﷻ for this replacement. The individuals or groups were the initiators of inviting and executing these spiritual cancerous cells in the person. Then, as sunnatullah required, the people technically killed themselves spiritually. New people with new healthy spiritual cells were replaced by Allah ﷻ.

One should remember that in the works of the dìn regardless of they are successful or not, those are the means and opportunities to please Allah ﷻ as mentioned وَلاَ تَضُرُّوهُ شَيْئًا. If Allah ﷻ wanted all the humans and Jinn truly could have recognized and appreciated Allah ﷻ as mentioned وَاللّهُ عَلَى كُلِّ شَيْءٍ قَدِيرٌ {39/التوبة}[112]. Yet, Allah ﷻ gives us opportunities such as dawah, tabligh or other good efforts and actions to use them as some means to please Allah ﷻ.

Allah ﷻ is Always Sufficient for the Genuine People/Ahlullah on the Path of Allah ﷻ

When we analyze the ayah[113] إِلاَّ تَنصُرُوهُ فَقَدْ نَصَرَهُ اللّهُ إِذْ أَخْرَجَهُ الَّذِينَ كَفَرُواْ ثَانِيَ اثْنَيْنِ إِذْ هُمَا فِي الْغَارِ إِذْ يَقُولُ لِصَاحِبِهِ لاَ تَحْزَنْ إِنَّ اللّهَ مَعَنَا فَأَنزَلَ اللّهُ سَكِينَتَهُ عَلَيْهِ

---

112. If you do not go forth, He will punish you with a painful punishment and will replace you with another people, and you will not harm Him at all. And Allah is over all things competent.
113. If you do not aid the Prophet - Allah has already aided him when those who disbelieved had driven him out [of Makkah] as one of two, when they were in the cave and he said to his companion, "Do not grieve; indeed Allah is with us." And Allah sent down his tranquillity upon him and supported him with angels you did not see and made the word of those who disbelieved the lowest, while the word of Allah - that is the highest. And Allah is Exalted in Might and Wise.

وَأَيَّدَهُ بِجُنُودٍ لَّمْ تَرَوْهَا وَجَعَلَ كَلِمَةَ الَّذِينَ كَفَرُواْ السُّفْلَى وَكَلِمَةُ اللهِ هِيَ الْعُلْيَا وَاللهُ عَزِيزٌ حَكِيمٌ {التوبة/40}, it is important to realize that sometimes we get discouraged by the negative, destructive and discouraging attitudes of people around us in the works of the dīn to please Allah ﷻ while we are trying to follow the path of Rasulullah ﷺ.

Yet, Allah ﷻ reminds us in the Qurān that Allah ﷻ is the One Who is the Real Helper as mentioned فَقَدْ نَصَرَهُ اللهُ. Yes, we need to seek help, act collectively, and engage others as a group as Allah ﷻ orders us to be with the people of good as Jama'ah. The barakah of Allah ﷻ is with the people of Jam'ah as mentioned by Rasulullah ﷺ.

Yet, when there are times that we are alone or left alone, then one should really remember that Allah ﷻ is the Real Helper as mentioned فَقَدْ نَصَرَهُ اللهُ. Humans are only means in this process to please Allah ﷻ. Yet, when these means become depleted or extinct, then one should really remember more at this time and all the times, the Real Helper and the Real One Who we seek the pleasure of. That is Allah ﷻ.

Sometimes numbers and achievements can really be another test to prevent and block the person about this reality. Then, these achievements or huge numbers of followers become a negative hindrance on the path of ikhlas to please Allah ﷻ.

One should remember that Allah ﷻ have different means of helping other than humans' apparent means of causalities as mentioned فَأَنزَلَ اللهُ سَكِينَتَهُ عَلَيْهِ وَأَيَّدَهُ بِجُنُودٍ لَّمْ تَرَوْهَا وَجَعَلَ كَلِمَةَ الَّذِينَ كَفَرُواْ السُّفْلَى وَكَلِمَةُ اللهِ هِيَ الْعُلْيَا وَاللهُ عَزِيزٌ حَكِيمٌ. Therefore, one should always and only seek the pleasure of Allah ﷻ on all walks of the life regardless of people's acceptance. Yet, trying to act as a group and being all inclusive, and not acting individualistic is the external dress. The internal dress is only acting, moving on and until the last breath working relentlessly to please only and always Allah ﷻ.

Allahumma Ja'lna minhum, Amīn.

Juz 14

Sûrah 17 al -Isrã

[23-24]

وَقَضَىٰ رَبُّكَ أَلَّا تَعْبُدُواْ إِلَّا إِيَّاهُ وَبِالْوَالِدَيْنِ إِحْسَانًا إِمَّا يَبْلُغَنَّ عِندَكَ الْكِبَرَ أَحَدُهُمَا أَوْ
كِلَاهُمَا فَلَا تَقُل لَّهُمَآ أُفٍّ وَلَا تَنْهَرْهُمَا وَقُل لَّهُمَا قَوْلاً كَرِيمًا {الإسراء/23} ¹¹⁴ وَاخْفِضْ
لَهُمَا جَنَاحَ الذُّلِّ مِنَ الرَّحْمَةِ وَقُل رَّبِّ ارْحَمْهُمَا كَمَا رَبَّيَانِي صَغِيرًا {الإسراء/24}

Old-Aged Parents

Allah ﷻ changes the responsibilities of human relations as part of the sunnatullah. When a child is dependent on the parents, after many years, the parents with an old age can be dependent on the children for their basic needs and bodily functions.

In these cases of sunnatullah, there can be very intrinsic dynamics one should be very sensitive and careful.

When the parents embody the full reliance on Allah ﷻ through weakness, and physical poverty, then they embody full tawakkul on Allah ﷻ sourced from La ilaha illa Allah before they meet with Rabbul Alamin. In other words, a person who experience the difficulties of old age actually can be getting trained and purified to only make tawakkul to Allah ﷻ with ikhlas and full tawhid before meeting with Allah ﷻ with death with the Grace, Fadl, and Rahmah of Allah ﷻ.

Yet, Allah ﷻ shows and sends us these signs as ayahs for everyone. The children have a sign for an internal reflection of the past memories with the parents when they were strong and now they are weak. The children then immediately foresee their own future with old age and weakness.

Yet, in this sunnatullah of old age with its difficulties for the parents, one of the tests and trials and removal of any type of shirk can be due to the parents' apparent or peripheral dependency on their own children.

---

114. And your Lord has decreed that you not worship except Him, and to parents, good treatment. Whether one or both of them reach old age [while] with you, say not to them [so much as], "uff," and do not repel them but speak to them a noble word. And lower to them the wing of humility out of mercy and say, "My Lord, have mercy upon them as they brought me up [when I was] small."

Their children who they have tried to raise now are trying to give them care. This position indeed can make the parents more sensitive that at a position of authority and care-giver, then they become in need as the person of need for care.

This is mentioned as يَبْلُغَنَّ عِندَكَ الْكِبَرَ أَحَدُهُمَا أَوْ كِلَاهُمَا فَلَا تَقُل لَّهُمَا أُفٍّ وَلَا تَنْهَرْهُمَا وَقُل لَّهُمَا قَوْلاً كَرِيمًا. At this position, the children do not take the position of authority over their parents but still maintain their humbleness, humility, and niceness while they are taking care of them as mentioned وَاخْفِضْ لَهُمَا جَنَاحَ الذُّلِّ مِنَ الرَّحْمَةِ.

Tawhid in Allah ﷻ and Parenthood & Childhood Institution

Allah ﷻ orders the right of parents after imān as mentioned وَقَضَى رَبُّكَ أَلاَّ تَعْبُدُواْ إِلاَّ إِيَّاهُ وَبِالْوَالِدَيْنِ إِحْسَانًا.

Yet, parents are still humans. Their right of the authority on the person is not comparable to the right and authority of Allah ﷻ.

Therefore, in the cycle of sunnatullah, as the creation of Allah ﷻ, both parents and children go through the cycles of weakness, strength and weakness as all are ab'd of Allah ﷻ as mentioned[115] اللَّهُ الَّذِي خَلَقَكُم مِّن ضَعْفٍ ثُمَّ جَعَلَ مِن بَعْدِ ضَعْفٍ قُوَّةً ثُمَّ جَعَلَ مِن بَعْدِ قُوَّةٍ ضَعْفًا وَشَيْبَةً يَخْلُقُ مَا يَشَاء وَهُوَ الْعَلِيمُ الْقَدِيرُ {الروم/54}.

This is another reality of difference of Allah ﷻ from the creation as mentioned[116] لْ هُوَ اللَّهُ أَحَدٌ {الإخلاص/1} اللَّهُ الصَّمَدُ {الإخلاص/2} لَمْ يَلِدْ وَلَمْ يُولَدْ {الإخلاص/3} وَلَمْ يَكُن لَّهُ كُفُوًا أَحَدٌ {الإخلاص/4}.

This is another reality of why parent or children attributions of humans to Allah ﷻ all human faulty constructions are.

Parenthood and childhood all indicate dependency. Children as weak creations from birth not able to walk are dependent on caregivers such as parents. Parents as weak individuals in old age are now dependent on children, welfare or other means. The whole notion of retirement systems and social security well ware is the outcome of the acceptance of dependency of humans in their old age to other means.

The One Who is Independent, doesn't have any children and parent, Only One, Unique, and nothing is similar is Allah ﷻ, Rabbul Alamìn.

---

115. Allah is the one who created you from weakness, then made after weakness strength, then made after strength weakness and white hair. He creates what He wills, and He is the Knowing, the Competent.
116. Say, "He is Allah, [who is] One, Allah, the Eternal Refuge. He neither begets nor is born, Nor is there to Him any equivalent."

To emphasize this point, everyone both parent and children have separate and individual accountability with Allah ﷻ as mentioned[117] وَوَالِدٍ

وَمَا وَلَدَ {البلد/3} لَقَدْ خَلَقْنَا الْإِنسَانَ فِي كَبَدٍ {البلد/4} أَيَحْسَبُ أَن لَّن يَقْدِرَ عَلَيْهِ أَحَدٌ {البلد/5}[118]

يَا أَيُّهَا النَّاسُ اتَّقُوا رَبَّكُمْ وَاخْشَوْا يَوْمًا لَّا يَجْزِي وَالِدٌ عَن وَلَدِهِ وَلَا مَوْلُودٌ هُوَ جَازٍ عَن and وَالِدِهِ شَيْئًا إِنَّ وَعْدَ اللَّهِ حَقٌّ فَلَا تَغُرَّنَّكُمُ الْحَيَاةُ الدُّنْيَا وَلَا يَغُرَّنَّكُم بِاللَّهِ الْغَرُورُ {لقمان/33}[119]

They are all 'abd of Allah ﷻ and everything understands this except some humans as mentioned[120] تَكَادُ السَّمَاوَاتُ يَتَفَطَّرْنَ مِنْهُ وَتَنشَقُّ الْأَرْضُ وَتَخِرُّ الْجِبَالُ هَدًّا {مريم/90} أَن دَعَوْا لِلرَّحْمَنِ وَلَدًا {مريم/91} وَمَا يَنبَغِي لِلرَّحْمَنِ أَن يَتَّخِذَ وَلَدًا {مريم/92} إِن كُلُّ مَن فِي السَّمَاوَاتِ وَالْأَرْضِ إِلَّا آتِي الرَّحْمَنِ عَبْدًا {مريم/93}

That is the primary relationship for the person, that is being a'bd of Allah ﷻ.

The titles of parents or being children are given by Allah ﷻ with the Divine Qadar. Each destined position has requirements and responsibilities that the person will be accountable in front of Rabbul Alamin Who is the Giver of All these Positions.

One of the required responsibilities is making dua to parents in this given Destined Qadar by Allah ﷻ as mentioned[121] وَقُل رَّبِّ ارْحَمْهُمَا كَمَا رَبَّيَانِي صَغِيرًا {الإسراء/24}

It is important to realize that the word رَّبِّ is used twice. We turn to Our Real Absolute and Only Real Rabb, رَّبِّ, Allah ﷻ to ask mercy, Rahmah and help for our parents who have the reflection of the shadow of the Attribute and Name of Allah ﷻ as Rabb as mentioned كَمَا رَبَّيَانِي صَغِيرًا.

Therefore, everyone and everything has a limited position when compared to our expected position with Rabbul Alamin.

Yes, seeing our parents in old age in need and weak can shatter our hearts.

---

117. And [by] the father and that which was born [of him], We have certainly created man into hardship.

118. Does he think that never will anyone overcome him?

119. O mankind, fear your Lord and fear a Day when no father will avail his son, nor will a son avail his father at all. Indeed, the promise of Allah is truth, so let not the worldly life delude you and be not deceived about Allah by the Deceiver.

120. The heavens almost rupture therefrom and the earth splits open and the mountains collapse in devastation That they attribute to the Most Merciful a son. And it is not appropriate for the Most Merciful that He should take a son. There is no one in the heavens and earth but that he comes to the Most Merciful as a servant.

121. And lower to them the wing of humility out of mercy and say, "My Lord, have mercy upon them as they brought me up [when I was] small."

Yes, being physically dependent our children when we are old can shatter our hearts.

Yet, all are shadow of the shadow . . . in their relation with All Hayy Qayyum, Ahad, al-Baki, al-Qadìr, Al-Rahman, Al-Rahim, Al-Karim, Rabbul Alamin, Allah ﷻ.

One can remember the hadith of Rasulullah ﷺ, when observing a mother in the battle field frantically looking for her son if he is dead or alive, and finally finding her son and relieving herself due to her mercy on him, and then, Rasulullah ﷺ mentions that Allah ﷻ has more Mercy, Rahmah with the a'bd when he or she sees turns to Allah ﷻ. Then, one can ask who has more mercy: our own loved ones, parents, mothers or fathers with their limited reflection of the Divine Attributes? Or, Allah ﷻ Who is Source of Rahmah, and Karam?

Allah ﷻ is the Source of All Infinite Rahmah and Karam. Rasulullah ﷺ is the first and the most one who reflects the utmost Rahmah of Allah ﷻ as the creation as mentioned[122] {الأنبياء/107} وَمَا أَرْسَلْنَاكَ إِلاَّ رَحْمَةً لِّلْعَالَمِينَ

Radina Billahi Rabba wa Bil Islami Dina wa bi Muhammadan Nabiyyan wa Rasula,

Raditu Billahi Rabba wa Bil ISlami Dina wa bi Muhammada Nabiyyan wa Rasula.

---

122. And We have not sent you, [O Muhammad], except as a mercy to the worlds.

Juz 15

Sûrah 18 al-Kahf

[60-65]

وَإِذْ قَالَ مُوسَى لِفَتَاهُ لَا أَبْرَحُ حَتَّى أَبْلُغَ مَجْمَعَ الْبَحْرَيْنِ أَوْ أَمْضِيَ حُقُبًا {الكهف/60}[123]

فَلَمَّا بَلَغَا مَجْمَعَ بَيْنِهِمَا نَسِيَا حُوتَهُمَا فَاتَّخَذَ سَبِيلَهُ فِي الْبَحْرِ سَرَبًا {الكهف/61}

فَلَمَّا جَاوَزَا قَالَ لِفَتَاهُ آتِنَا غَدَاءنَا لَقَدْ لَقِينَا مِن سَفَرِنَا هَذَا نَصَبًا {الكهف/62}[124] قَالَ أَرَأَيْتَ إِذْ أَوَيْنَا إِلَى الصَّخْرَةِ فَإِنِّي نَسِيتُ الْحُوتَ وَمَا أَنسَانِيهُ إِلَّا الشَّيْطَانُ أَنْ أَذْكُرَهُ وَاتَّخَذَ سَبِيلَهُ فِي الْبَحْرِ عَجَبًا {الكهف/63} قَالَ ذَلِكَ مَا كُنَّا نَبْغِ فَارْتَدَّا عَلَى آثَارِهِمَا قَصَصًا {الكهف/64} فَوَجَدَا عَبْدًا مِّنْ عِبَادِنَا آتَيْنَاهُ رَحْمَةً مِنْ عِندِنَا وَعَلَّمْنَاهُ مِن لَّدُنَّا عِلْمًا {الكهف/8}

Education & Training: Youth

When we look at the above ayahs in the perspectives of concepts around the word لِفَتَاهُ, one can focus on the notions of interaction, education and training related with the youth.

It is important help to raise generation that would carry the work of Allah ﷻ in teaching and reminding people the guidelines of the Qurān and sunnah of Rasulullah ﷺ.

Sometimes, the realities of youth necessitate both formal classical education and adventurous experiential engagements of traveling. Youth have energy to discharge themselves. When this is combined with the teachings of the Qurān and Rasulullah ﷺ, then there can be permanent effects on the personalities of the youth.

Today's youth camps underline this practice even for the secular minded people to engage young people with adventure.

---

123. And [mention] when Moses said to his servant, "I will not cease [traveling] until I reach the junction of the two seas or continue for a long period." But when they reached the junction between them, they forgot their fish, and it took its course into the sea, slipping away.

124. So when they had passed beyond it, [Moses] said to his boy, "Bring us our morning meal. We have certainly suffered in this, our journey, [much] fatigue." He said, "Did you see when we retired to the rock? Indeed, I forgot [there] the fish. And none made me forget it except Satan - that I should mention it. And it took its course into the sea amazingly". [Moses] said, "That is what we were seeking." So they returned, following their footprints. And they found a servant from among Our servants to whom we had given mercy from us and had taught him from Us a [certain] knowledge.

In this regard, Musa as had a young person referred as لِفَتَاهُ. In the tafāsir, it is mentioned that this young man was Yusha as who led the Ban-i Israel after Musa as.

In this regard, Musa as's engagement with Yusha in traveling as can indicate this educational and training perspective.

It is interesting to note that after Musa as meets with Khidr as there is no mention of Yusha as in the story.

In this case, now, Musa as takes the position of a student next to Khidr as to be trained and educated about a specific knowledge. Again, in this case, their training and education experience are embedded in a traveling experience.

One can see that traveling and education-learning have a positive relationship to help the person to detach themselves from their habitat and to focus on the content of the knowledge in an unfamiliar habitat with the experience of traveling.

Juz 16

Sûrah 18 al-Kahf

[85, 89 & 92]

فَأَتْبَعَ سَبَبًا {الكهف/85}[125]

ثُمَّ أَتْبَعَ سَبَبًا {الكهف/98}[126]

ثُمَّ أَتْبَعَ سَبَبًا {الكهف/92}[127]

When we analyze the above ayahs, besides their many meanings, one can realize that there is the rûh, spirit of chivalry in Zul-Qarnayn. This spirit makes him to help people and standing against injustice and oppression.

On the other hand, we try to find means in this short span of life to please Allah ﷻ. The word سَبَبًا can indicate different means that we run behind to please Allah ﷻ.

When one reviews the life of Rasulullah ﷺ, his life was full of these means. In other words, Rasulullah ﷺ embodied ihsan and all his

125. So he followed a way
126. Then he followed a way
127. Then he followed a way

minutes, seconds and hours in his life span had a means to please Allah
﷾.

One can remember a lot of incidents in his life to use all the means
as an opportunity to please Allah ﷾. Rasulullah ﷺ had the embodiment
of chivalry in the positive, encouraging, and active way of always being
in the service of people.

It is important to revive this sunnah of Rasulullah ﷺ at especially
these times when people are running away from means of responsibilities,
and doing work to please Allah ﷾ due to laziness, demotivational
attitudes and pessimism. May Allah SWT protect us, Amìn.

Juz 18

Sûrah 23 al-Mu'minûn

[12-16]

Statistical Arguments & Lost Wanderer Scientists

وَلَقَدْ خَلَقْنَا الْإِنسَانَ مِن سُلَالَةٍ مِّن طِينٍ {المؤمنون/12} [128] ثُمَّ جَعَلْنَاهُ نُطْفَةً فِي قَرَارٍ
مَّكِينٍ {المؤمنون/13} ثُمَّ خَلَقْنَا النُّطْفَةَ عَلَقَةً فَخَلَقْنَا الْعَلَقَةَ مُضْغَةً فَخَلَقْنَا الْمُضْغَةَ عِظَامًا
فَكَسَوْنَا الْعِظَامَ لَحْمًا ثُمَّ أَنشَأْنَاهُ خَلْقًا آخَرَ فَتَبَارَكَ اللَّهُ أَحْسَنُ الْخَالِقِينَ {المؤمنون/14}
ثُمَّ إِنَّكُم بَعْدَ ذَلِكَ لَمَيِّتُونَ {المؤمنون/15} ثُمَّ إِنَّكُمْ يَوْمَ الْقِيَامَةِ تُبْعَثُونَ {المؤمنون/16}

One should remember that nothing happens randomly or statistically
or haphazardly or by chance. Allah ﷾ wills with Divine Mashiyyah and
creates how ever and when ever and what ever Allah ﷾ wants to create
and to bring nothing from non-existence into something of existence.

This Divine Mashiyyah, Divine Iradah, Divine Qudrad are all
emphasized and repeated with the expressions

and وَلَقَدْ خَلَقْنَا الْإِنسَانَ
and ثُمَّ جَعَلْنَاهُ نُطْفَةً
and ثُمَّ خَلَقْنَا النُّطْفَةَ عَلَقَةً

---

128. And certainly did We create man from an extract of clay. Then We placed him as a sperm-
drop in a firm lodging. Then We made the sperm-drop into a clinging clot, and We made the
clot into a lump [of flesh], and We made [from] the lump, bones, and We covered the bones
with flesh; then We developed him into another creation. So blessed is Allah, the best of
creators. Then indeed, after that you are to die. Then indeed you, on the Day of Resurrection,
will be resurrected.

فَخَلَقْنَا الْعَلَقَةَ مُضْغَةً and
فَخَلَقْنَا الْمُضْغَةَ عِظَامًا and
فَكَسَوْنَا الْعِظَامَ لَحْمًا and
ثُمَّ أَنشَأْنَاهُ خَلْقًا آخَرَ

When one reviews above repeated terms with the word خَلَقْنَا, Allah
۩ could have used once this word خَلَقْنَا, and make atf, connection to
the other sentences. Yet, the word and the fi'il – verb خَلَقْنَا is repeated
constantly.

The repetition of the word خَلَقْنَا emphasize the Divine Mashiyyah,
Divine Iradah, Divine Qudrad of Allah ۩.

In other words, when we consider a human body, it is formed of
billions of atoms, today's science terminologies can classify to form
groups of enlarging scales compounds, amino acids, protein, DNA,
nucleus, cell, organism, bacteria, tissue, organ, systems and body.

The ayah can indicate the process of change at the subatomic and
atomic levels with the expression وَلَقَدْ خَلَقْنَا الْإِنسَانَ مِن سُلَالَةٍ مِّن سُلَالَةٍ in[129] مِن
طِينٍ {المؤمنون/12}. This change can indicate this subatomic and atomic
levels of processes at the earthly elemental levels referred in periodic
table of elements as mentioned with the word طِينٍ. In this regard the
sequence of formations such as the electrons, protons, mesons, baryons,
neutrons forming the specific periodic table elements, then them
forming compounds, then compounds forming structures of amino
acids such as DNA or RNA and then these materials being part of a cell
such as sperm cell referred as spermatozoon can be call part of the مِن
سُلَالَةٍ مِّن طِينٍ. Arabic word سُلَالَةٍ indicate sequential change and process.
Especially when this word is combined with the harf-jar مِّن in Arabic,
then there can be an emphasis in sequential process, Allahu A'lam.

In this regard, the choice of the word خَلَقْنَا can indicate the direct
Divine Creation in the process and the word جَعَلْنَاهُ can indicate the
causal intervention of the Divine Creation in the process as a reflection.

The plural form نا in both words can indicate the Majestic Divine
authority as well the intermediator agents/messengers such as the angels
in different perspectives of the direct and causal mediation of the giving
the news of the Divine Creation in the process.

---

129. And certainly did We create man from an extract of clay.

{ فَاتَّخَذَتْ مِن دُونِهِمْ حِجَابًا فَأَرْسَلْنَا إِلَيْهَا رُوحَنَا This can be mentioned in[130] فَتَمَثَّلَ لَهَا بَشَرًا سَوِيًّا {مريم/17} قَالَتْ إِنِّي أَعُوذُ بِالرَّحْمَن مِنكَ إِن كُنتَ تَقِيًّا {مريم/18} قَالَ إِنَّمَا أَنَا رَسُولُ رَبِّكِ لِأَهَبَ لَكِ غُلَامًا زَكِيًّا {مريم/19}

هَلْ أَتَاكَ حَدِيثُ ضَيْفِ إِبْرَاهِيمَ الْمُكْرَمِينَ {الذاريات/24}[131] إِذْ دَخَلُوا عَلَيْهِ فَقَالُوا سَلَامًا قَالَ سَلَامٌ قَوْمٌ مُّنكَرُونَ {الذاريات/25} فَرَاغَ إِلَى أَهْلِهِ فَجَاء بِعِجْلٍ سَمِينٍ {الذاريات/26} فَقَرَّبَهُ إِلَيْهِمْ قَالَ أَلَا تَأْكُلُونَ {الذاريات/27} فَأَوْجَسَ مِنْهُمْ خِيفَةً قَالُوا لَا تَخَفْ وَبَشَّرُوهُ بِغُلَامٍ عَلِيمٍ {الذاريات/28} فَأَقْبَلَتِ امْرَأَتُهُ فِي صَرَّةٍ فَصَكَّتْ وَجْهَهَا وَقَالَتْ عَجُوزٌ عَقِيمٌ {الذاريات/29}

Yet, intermediation is all means and reflections.

The Real Doer and Creator is Allah ﷻ in the Absolute Reality.

Then, the bigger structures in after fertilization of sperm and egg can include the processes of nutfah, and others as mentioned in the ayah.

Regardless of how the changing scientific terms call them, the essence of this formation is executed and ordered with the Divine Mashiyyah, Divine Iradah, Divine Qudrad of Allah ﷻ.

This is expressed as[132] إِنَّمَا أَمْرُهُ إِذَا أَرَادَ شَيْئًا أَنْ يَقُولَ لَهُ كُنْ فَيَكُونُ {يس/82}.

In other words, when Allah ﷻ mentions this repetition of the word خَلَقْنَا, it is to prevent humans' fallacies to be lost in the means referred as science and scientific laws but to emphasize the Divine Mashiyyah, Divine Iradah, Divine Qudrad of Allah ﷻ.

All the atoms in a cell ordered by Allah ﷻ to form a cell. These elements or atoms such as Hydrogen, Oxygen and others all in the earth mentioned with the word طِين as mentioned وَلَقَدْ خَلَقْنَا الْإِنسَانَ مِن سُلَالَةٍ مِّن طِينٍ. In the sense, periodic table including all the elements or atoms can be indicated with one-word طِين.

Yet, rather than only concentrating in the ingredients, a scientist gets lost and wanders through the impossible statistical arguments of possibilities to find a meaning of "how, when or why a specific atom

---

130. And We have created above you seven layered heavens, and never have We been of [Our] creation unaware. And We have sent down rain from the sky in a measured amount and settled it in the earth. And indeed, We are Able to take it away. And We brought forth for you thereby gardens of palm trees and grapevines in which for you are abundant fruits and from which you eat.

131. Has there reached you the story of the honored guests of Abraham? - When they entered upon him and said, "[We greet you with] peace." He answered, "[And upon you] peace, [you are] a people unknown. Then he went to his family and came with a fat [roasted] calf And placed it near them; he said, "Will you not eat?" And he felt from them apprehension. They said, "Fear not," and gave him good tidings of a learned boy. And his wife approached with a cry [of alarm] and struck her face and said, "[I am] a barren old woman!"

132. His command is only when He intends a thing that He says to it, "Be," and it is.

is assigned to a specific cell, DNA, nucleus, organism, bacteria, tissue, organ or body?"

They see this perfect and complex system and get amazed yet they get lost to end the journey of the means called science with a purposeful, understandable and clear ends.

The answer and the ends is very simple and straightforward that is La ilaha illa Allah.

Allah ﷻ is the One Who Wills, Originates, Creates, Forms, Designs, Executes, Chooses, and Orders each atom and they form a perfect, harmonious, and complex billions of systems as mentioned فَتَبَارَكَ اللهُ أَحْسَنُ الْخَالِقِينَ. SubhanAllah!

فَسُبْحَانَ اللَّهِ حِينَ تُمْسُونَ وَحِينَ تُصْبِحُونَ {الروم/17}[133] وَلَهُ الْحَمْدُ فِي السَّمَاوَاتِ وَالْأَرْضِ وَعَشِيًّا وَحِينَ تُظْهِرُونَ {الروم/18} يُخْرِجُ الْحَيَّ مِنَ الْمَيِّتِ وَيُخْرِجُ الْمَيِّتَ مِنَ الْحَيِّ وَيُحْيِي الْأَرْضَ بَعْدَ مَوْتِهَا وَكَذَلِكَ تُخْرَجُونَ {الروم/19} وَمِنْ آيَاتِهِ أَنْ خَلَقَكُم مِّن تُرَابٍ ثُمَّ إِذَا أَنتُم بَشَرٌ تَنتَشِرُونَ {الروم/20} وَمِنْ آيَاتِهِ أَنْ خَلَقَ لَكُم مِّنْ أَنفُسِكُمْ أَزْوَاجًا لِّتَسْكُنُوا إِلَيْهَا وَجَعَلَ بَيْنَكُم مَّوَدَّةً وَرَحْمَةً إِنَّ فِي ذَلِكَ لَآيَاتٍ لِّقَوْمٍ يَتَفَكَّرُونَ {الروم/21} وَمِنْ آيَاتِهِ خَلْقُ السَّمَاوَاتِ وَالْأَرْضِ وَاخْتِلَافُ أَلْسِنَتِكُمْ وَأَلْوَانِكُمْ إِنَّ فِي ذَلِكَ لَآيَاتٍ لِّلْعَالِمِينَ {الروم/22} وَمِنْ آيَاتِهِ مَنَامُكُم بِاللَّيْلِ وَالنَّهَارِ وَابْتِغَاؤُكُم مِّن فَضْلِهِ إِنَّ فِي ذَلِكَ لَآيَاتٍ لِّقَوْمٍ يَسْمَعُونَ {الروم/23} وَمِنْ آيَاتِهِ يُرِيكُمُ الْبَرْقَ خَوْفًا وَطَمَعًا وَيُنَزِّلُ مِنَ السَّمَاء مَاء فَيُحْيِي بِهِ الْأَرْضَ بَعْدَ مَوْتِهَا إِنَّ فِي ذَلِكَ لَآيَاتٍ لِّقَوْمٍ يَعْقِلُونَ {الروم/24}

وَمِنْ آيَاتِهِ أَن تَقُومَ السَّمَاء وَالْأَرْضُ بِأَمْرِهِ ثُمَّ إِذَا دَعَاكُمْ دَعْوَةً مِّنَ الْأَرْضِ إِذَا أَنتُمْ تَخْرُجُونَ {الروم/25} وَلَهُ مَن فِي السَّمَاوَاتِ وَالْأَرْضِ كُلٌّ لَّهُ قَانِتُونَ {الروم/26} وَهُوَ

---

133. So exalted is Allah when you reach the evening and when you reach the morning. And to Him is [due all] praise throughout the heavens and the earth. And [exalted is He] at night and when you are at noon. He brings the living out of the dead and brings the dead out of the living and brings to life the earth after its lifelessness. And thus will you be brought out. And of His signs is that He created you from dust; then, suddenly you were human beings dispersing [throughout the earth]. And of His signs is that He created for you from yourselves mates that you may find tranquillity in them; and He placed between you affection and mercy. Indeed in that are signs for a people who give thought. And of His signs is the creation of the heavens and the earth and the diversity of your languages and your colors. Indeed in that are signs for those of knowledge. And of His signs is your sleep by night and day and your seeking of His bounty. Indeed in that are signs for a people who listen. And of His signs is [that] He shows you the lightning [causing] fear and aspiration, and He sends down rain from the sky by which He brings to life the earth after its lifelessness. Indeed in that are signs for a people who use reason. And of His signs is that the heaven and earth remain by His command. Then when He calls you with a [single] call from the earth, immediately you will come forth. And to Him belongs whoever is in the heavens and earth. All are to Him devoutly obedient. And it is He who begins creation; then He repeats it, and that is [even] easier for Him. To Him belongs the highest attribute in the heavens and earth. And He is the Exalted in Might, the Wise.

الَّذِي يَبْدَأُ الْخَلْقَ ثُمَّ يُعِيدُهُ وَهُوَ أَهْوَنُ عَلَيْهِ وَلَهُ الْمَثَلُ الْأَعْلَى فِي السَّمَاوَاتِ وَالْأَرْضِ وَهُوَ
الْعَزِيزُ الْحَكِيمُ {الروم/27} ضَرَبَ لَكُم مَّثَلًا مِنْ أَنفُسِكُمْ هَل لَّكُم مِّن مَّا مَلَكَتْ أَيْمَانُكُم
مِّن شُرَكَاء فِي مَا رَزَقْنَاكُمْ فَأَنتُمْ فِيهِ سَوَاء تَخَافُونَهُمْ كَخِيفَتِكُمْ أَنفُسَكُمْ كَذَلِكَ نُفَصِّلُ الْآيَاتِ
لِقَوْمٍ يَعْقِلُونَ {الروم/28} [134 بَلِ اتَّبَعَ الَّذِينَ ظَلَمُوا أَهْوَاءهُم بِغَيْرِ عِلْمٍ فَمَن يَهْدِي مَنْ أَضَلَّ
اللَّهُ وَمَا لَهُم مِّن نَّاصِرِينَ {الروم/29} [135 فَأَقِمْ وَجْهَكَ لِلدِّينِ حَنِيفًا فِطْرَةَ اللَّهِ الَّتِي فَطَرَ
النَّاسَ عَلَيْهَا لَا تَبْدِيلَ لِخَلْقِ اللَّهِ ذَلِكَ الدِّينُ الْقَيِّمُ وَلَكِنَّ أَكْثَرَ النَّاسِ لَا يَعْلَمُونَ {الروم/30}
مُنِيبِينَ إِلَيْهِ وَاتَّقُوهُ وَأَقِيمُوا الصَّلَاةَ وَلَا تَكُونُوا مِنَ الْمُشْرِكِينَ {الروم/31} مِنَ الَّذِينَ
فَرَّقُوا دِينَهُمْ وَكَانُوا شِيَعًا كُلُّ حِزْبٍ بِمَا لَدَيْهِمْ فَرِحُونَ {الروم/32}

After all the above ayahs, who can say anything to conclude except
another ayah as[136] وَقُلْ جَاء الْحَقُّ وَزَهَقَ الْبَاطِلُ إِنَّ الْبَاطِلَ كَانَ زَهُوقًا {الإسراء/81}
and [137]بَلْ نَقْذِفُ بِالْحَقِّ عَلَى الْبَاطِلِ فَيَدْمَغُهُ فَإِذَا هُوَ زَاهِقٌ وَلَكُمُ الْوَيْلُ مِمَّا تَصِفُونَ {الأنبياء/18}

Juz 22

Sûrah 33

[41]

[138]يَا أَيُّهَا الَّذِينَ آمَنُوا اذْكُرُوا اللَّهَ ذِكْرًا كَثِيرًا {الأحزاب/41}

Dhikrullah–The Essence of Imān

One of the main essences of imān is dhikr-remembrance of Allah ﷻ.
Gatherings, meetings and even things done on the path of Allah ﷻ and

---

134. He presents to you an example from yourselves. Do you have among those whom your
right hands possess any partners in what We have provided for you so that you are equal
therein [and] would fear them as your fear of one another [within a partnership]? Thus do We
detail the verses for a people who use reason.
135. But those who wrong follow their [own] desires without knowledge. Then who can
guide one whom Allah has sent astray? And for them there are no helpers. So direct your
face toward the religion, inclining to truth. [Adhere to] the fitrah of Allah upon which He has
created [all] people. No change should there be in the creation of Allah. That is the correct
religion, but most of the people do not know. [Adhere to it], turning in repentance to Him,
and fear Him and establish prayer and do not be of those who associate others with Allah [Or]
of those who have divided their religion and become sects, every faction rejoicing in what it
has.
136. And say, "Truth has come, and falsehood has departed. Indeed is falsehood, [by nature],
ever bound to depart."
137. Rather, We dash the truth upon falsehood, and it destroys it, and thereupon it departs.
And for you is destruction from that which you describe.
138. O you who have believed, remember Allah with much remembrance

for the sake of Allah ﷻ without the dhikr of Allah ﷻ would be without barakah, temporary and not effective.

When we engage in any transaction as a person of imān, if there is the absence of Dhikrullah either through the dua of istikhara or other means, that transaction will not have any barakah and would be abtar-unfruitful.

My heart and our hearts calm down and settle in peace only but only with Dhikrullah-remembrance of Allah ﷻ as mentioned[139] الَّذِينَ آمَنُواْ وَتَطْمَئِنُّ قُلُوبُهُم بِذِكْرِ اللَّهِ أَلاَ بِذِكْرِ اللَّهِ تَطْمَئِنُّ الْقُلُوبُ {الرعد/28}

The absence of Dhikrullah causes contractions and solidification of the hearts as mentioned[140] أَفَمَن شَرَحَ اللَّهُ صَدْرَهُ لِلْإِسْلاَمِ فَهُوَ عَلَى نُورٍ مِّن رَّبِّهِ فَوَيْلٌ لِّلْقَاسِيَةِ قُلُوبُهُم مِّن ذِكْرِ اللَّهِ أُوْلَئِكَ فِي ضَلاَلٍ مُبِينٍ {الزمر/22}.

اللَّهُ نَزَّلَ أَحْسَنَ الْحَدِيثِ كِتَابًا مُّتَشَابِهًا مَّثَانِيَ تَقْشَعِرُّ مِنْهُ جُلُودُ الَّذِينَ يَخْشَوْنَ رَبَّهُمْ ثُمَّ تَلِينُ جُلُودُهُمْ وَقُلُوبُهُمْ إِلَى ذِكْرِ اللَّهِ ذَلِكَ هُدَى اللَّهِ يَهْدِي بِهِ مَنْ يَشَاء وَمَن يُضْلِلْ اللَّهُ فَمَا لَهُ مِنْ هَادٍ {الزمر/23} أَفَمَن يَتَّقِي بِوَجْهِهِ سُوءَ الْعَذَابِ يَوْمَ الْقِيَامَةِ وَقِيلَ لِلظَّالِمِينَ ذُوقُوا مَا كُنتُمْ تَكْسِبُونَ {الزمر/24}

In this regard, any gathering or a place of gathering that implements Dhikrullah is transformed into a place of barakah, sakinah-calmness, and tranquility as mentioned[141]

فِي بُيُوتٍ أَذِنَ اللَّهُ أَن تُرْفَعَ وَيُذْكَرَ فِيهَا اسْمُهُ يُسَبِّحُ لَهُ فِيهَا بِالْغُدُوِّ وَالْآصَالِ {النور/36}

رِجَالٌ لَّا تُلْهِيهِمْ تِجَارَةٌ وَلَا بَيْعٌ عَن ذِكْرِ اللَّهِ وَإِقَامِ الصَّلَاةِ وَإِيتَاء الزَّكَاةِ يَخَافُونَ يَوْمًا تَتَقَلَّبُ فِيهِ الْقُلُوبُ وَالْأَبْصَارُ {النور/37}[142]

---

139. Those who have believed and whose hearts are assured by the remembrance of Allah. Unquestionably, by the remembrance of Allah hearts are assured."
140. So is one whose breast Allah has expanded to [accept] Islam and he is upon a light from his Lord [like one whose heart rejects it]? Then woe to those whose hearts are hardened against the remembrance of Allah. Those are in manifest error. Allah has sent down the best statement: a consistent Book wherein is reiteration. The skins shiver therefrom of those who fear their Lord; then their skins and their hearts relax at the remembrance of Allah. That is the guidance of Allah by which He guides whom He wills. And one whom Allah leaves astray - for him there is no guide. Then is he who will shield with his face the worst of the punishment on the Day of Resurrection [like one secure from it]? And it will be said to the wrongdoers, "Taste what you used to earn."
141. [Such niches are] in mosques which Allah has ordered to be raised and that His name be mentioned therein; exalting Him within them in the morning and the evenings
142. [Are] men whom neither commerce nor sale distracts from the remembrance of Allah and performance of prayer and giving of zakah. They fear a Day in which the hearts and eyes will [fearfully] turn about -

One should remember that it is the Grace, Fadl, and Karam of Allah ﷻ that Allah ﷻ enables these fortunate ones as mentioned with the expression فِي بُيُوتٍ أَذِنَ اللَّهُ أَنْ تُرْفَعَ وَيُذْكَرَ فِيهَا اسْمُهُ أَذِنَ اللَّهُ in. Yes, being in the gatherings of remembrance of Allah-Dhikrullah and being one of the people who remembers Allah ﷻ is itself a blessing and ni'mah from Allah ﷻ.

These are the real men-fatā and have the means of futuwwah-chivalry as mentioned with the word رِجَالٌ.

Allahumma A'inna A'la Dhikrika Wa Shukrika Wa Husni I'badatik, Amìn.

Personal and Collective Dhikrullah

One should remember that ihsān requires that we embody the Dhikrullah at all times and at all places. The embodiment of Dhikrullah, Rasulullah ﷺ , al-Habìb ﷺ mentions that even he ﷺ embodies Dhikrullah in his blessed sleep ﷺ [3][143].

The highest forms of personal required Dhikrullah is five-times salah at any place at the required intervals. Yet, this personal required Dhikrullah reaches at a higher level when it is performed in Jam'ah and in the masjid by following the sunnah of Rasulullah ﷺ.

The highest forms of collective required Dhikrullah is salatul-Juma'. This required Dhikrullah has a specific time and place as mentioned[144] يَا أَيُّهَا الَّذِينَ آمَنُوا إِذَا نُودِيَ لِلصَّلَاةِ مِنْ يَوْمِ الْجُمُعَةِ فَاسْعَوْا إِلَى ذِكْرِ اللَّهِ وَذَرُوا الْبَيْعَ ذَلِكُمْ خَيْرٌ لَكُمْ إِنْ كُنْتُمْ تَعْلَمُونَ {الجمعة/9}.

Other forms of encouraged and boosting personal Dhikrullah are the ones primarily performed first by Rasulullah ﷺ, then sahabah, tabi'un and other pious salaf.

Other forms of encouraged and boosting collective Dhikrullah are the ones primarily performed first by Rasulullah ﷺ, then sahabah, tabi'un and other pious salaf.

Some of the pious salaf established structures and systems to make the Dhikrullah easier in collective and personal practices by systemizing and extrapolating the sunnah of Rasulullah ﷺ and the sahabah, and

143. Hadith #138
144. O you who have believed, when [the adhan] is called for the prayer on the day of Jumu'ah [Friday], then proceed to the remembrance of Allah and leave trade. That is better for you, if you only knew.

tabi'un. The schools of tasawwuf such as Nakshibandi, Chisti, or others are all examples of these blessings as long as people genuinely follow them with the intention and under the guidelines of following the Qurān and Sunnah of Rasulullah ﷺ, al-Habìb ﷺ.

[69-70]

Negative Attitudes, Negative Criticism & Fault-Finding

يَا أَيُّهَا الَّذِينَ آمَنُوا لَا تَكُونُوا كَالَّذِينَ آذَوْا مُوسَى فَبَرَّأَهُ اللَّهُ مِمَّا قَالُوا وَكَانَ عِندَ اللَّهِ وَجِيهًا {الأحزاب/69}¹⁴⁵ يَا أَيُّهَا الَّذِينَ آمَنُوا اتَّقُوا اللَّه وَقُولُوا قَوْلاً سَدِيدًا {الأحزاب/70}

One of the critical dynamics uniting people is their positive attitude of unification but not promoting conflict, fault-finding, negative criticism and separation.

When a person or people are at the position of uniting others with positive attitudes, there will be still ones who may cause spiritual and mental pain through their negative attitudes as mentioned with the word آذَوْا.

Sometimes, this pain can be caused by good intentioned people due to lack of adab, etiquette or absence of usul or methodology of positive or constructive communication.

Sometimes, this pain can be caused by ill-intentioned people regardless of how they may be referred as munafiqs, kafir and others with spiritual diseased hearts.

Yet, since these people are in realities of our lives, one can try to ignore them, sometimes still try to work with them although it can be very painful.

One of the possible reasons why Musa as is one of the ulul-azm prophets is that he as was working with some of his people who were constantly giving him آذَوْا as mentioned here يَا أَيُّهَا الَّذِينَ آمَنُوا لَا تَكُونُوا كَالَّذِينَ قَالُوا يَا مُوسَى إِنَّا لَن نَّدْخُلَهَا أَبَدًا مَّا دَامُوا فِيهَا فَاذْهَبْ and other places as¹⁴⁶ آذَوْا مُوسَى أَنتَ وَرَبُّكَ فَقَاتِلا إِنَّا هَاهُنَا قَاعِدُونَ {المائدة/24}

---

145. O you who have believed, be not like those who abused Moses; then Allah cleared him of what they said. And he, in the sight of Allah, was distinguished. O you who have believed, fear Allah and speak words of appropriate justice.

146. They said, "O Moses, indeed we will not enter it, ever, as long as they are within it; so go, you and your Lord, and fight. Indeed, we are remaining right here."

There were also times and incidents these type of negative attitudes during the time of Rasulullah ﷺ as is mentioned as[147] يَمُنُّونَ عَلَيْكَ أَنْ أَسْلَمُوا قُل لَّا تَمُنُّوا عَلَيَّ إِسْلَامَكُم بَلِ اللَّهُ يَمُنُّ عَلَيْكُمْ أَنْ هَدَاكُمْ لِلْإِيمَانِ إِن كُنتُمْ صَادِقِينَ {الحجرات/17} or سَلَقُوكُم بِأَلْسِنَةٍ حِدَادٍ أَشِحَّةً عَلَى الْخَيْرِ أُولَٰئِكَ لَمْ يُؤْمِنُوا فَأَحْبَطَ اللَّهُ أَعْمَالَهُمْ وَكَانَ ذَٰلِكَ عَلَى اللَّهِ يَسِيرًا {الأحزاب/19}[148].

One should remember that a believer of Allah ﷻ with imān should always embody the positive, gentle and kind and constructive form of verbal engagement as mentioned[149] يَا أَيُّهَا الَّذِينَ آمَنُوا اتَّقُوا اللَّهَ وَقُولُوا قَوْلًا سَدِيدًا {الأحزاب/70}. The expression قَوْلًا سَدِيدًا can indicate this positive and constructive approaches of promoting unification in verbal engagements.

Most of the time, we are discouraged by the people around us due to this absence of positive constructive and encouraging attitudes of doing good-khayr. Yes, one should also correct themselves with advices. Yet, our realities require that we need constructive advices with positive and well-intended engagements.

In the absence of this positive attitudes, one way can be separation from the people who give difficulty as mentioned with آذَوْا through their words, statements or engagements as mentioned يَمُنُّونَ عَلَيْكَ أَنْ أَسْلَمُوا or سَلَقُوكُم بِأَلْسِنَةٍ حِدَادٍ.

The other default position can be maintaining to be with the people, bearing and enduring their harsh treatments as this was the case most or all the time with the prophets of Allah ﷻ.

Profits, Loss & Gains

Yes, today's popularized trends of books or approaches on conflict resolution, working with difficult people, and management, giving perspectives mostly in business or corporate world how to maintain a profit for the company by minimizing these conflicts.

---

147. They consider it a favor to you that they have accepted Islam. Say, "Do not consider your Islam a favor to me. Rather, Allah has conferred favor upon you that He has guided you to the faith, if you should be truthful."

148. Indisposed toward you. And when fear comes, you see them looking at you, their eyes revolving like one being overcome by death. But when fear departs, they lash you with sharp tongues, indisposed toward [any] good. Those have not believed, so Allah has rendered their deeds worthless, and ever is that, for Allah, easy.

149. O you who have believed, fear Allah and speak words of appropriate justice.

Similarly, in the works of the dīn, a similar approach can be adapted to please Allah ﷻ with taqwa as mentioned يَا أَيُّهَا الَّذِينَ آمَنُوا اتَّقُوا اللَّهَ وَقُولُوا قَوْلًا سَدِيدًا {الأحزاب/70}. Yet, the intention here is to promote unification by not oversizing and overthinking about belligerent and vulgar attitudes of people but moving on for a higher goal for saving people from Jahannam in the engagements of imān in order to please Allah ﷻ.

Sometimes, if we get lost in peripheral issues of people's negative attitudes, then we lose the real motivation of why we exist, our purpose in life, and why we engage with what we engage.

If this perspective of focusing on the main goal is adapted, then one can move on for the sake of Allah ﷻ due this higher goal in the clashes between spouses, between the coworkers in a company and between the clashes, conflicts and all belligerent attitudes in the works of the dīn for the sake of Allah ﷻ.

This is called taqwa as mentioned[150] يَا أَيُّهَا الَّذِينَ آمَنُوا اتَّقُوا اللَّهَ وَقُولُوا قَوْلًا سَدِيدًا {الأحزاب/70}

May Allah ﷻ always keep our perspectives, goals, intentions in the reality of pleasing Allah ﷻ by making our goal saving people's imān but not sidetracked on the secondary and peripheral issues, Amīn.

Taqwa is the key for the Acceptance and Pleasure of Allah ﷻ

One should realize that taqwa is the acceptance of all amal, works and efforts on the path of Allah ﷻ. It is not the intelligence of people, and how much what they say is correct, always to the point and they are very influential. It is the positive and constructive attitudes of people sourced from taqwa.

If we continue to analyze the case of Musa as when his people used this expression, then

Allah ﷻ gives another example of on the continuation of the same topic as mentioned[151] قَالُواْ يَا مُوسَى إِنَّا لَن نَّدْخُلَهَا أَبَدًا مَّا دَامُواْ فِيهَا فَاذْهَبْ أَنتَ وَرَبُّكَ فَقَاتِلا إِنَّا هَاهُنَا قَاعِدُونَ {المائدة/24} قَالَ رَبِّ إِنِّي لا أَمْلِكُ إِلاَّ نَفْسِي وَأَخِي فَافْرُقْ بَيْنَنَا وَبَيْنَ الْقَوْمِ الْفَاسِقِينَ {المائدة/25} قَالَ فَإِنَّهَا مُحَرَّمَةٌ عَلَيْهِمْ أَرْبَعِينَ سَنَةً يَتِيهُونَ فِي الأَرْضِ فَلاَ تَأْسَ

---

150. O you who have believed, fear Allah and speak words of appropriate justice.
151. They said, "O Moses, indeed we will not enter it, ever, as long as they are within it; so go, you and your Lord, and fight. Indeed, we are remaining right here."

عَلَى الْقَوْمِ الْفَاسِقِينَ {المائدة/26} ¹⁵² وَاتْلُ عَلَيْهِمْ نَبَأَ ابْنَيْ آدَمَ بِالْحَقِّ إِذْ قَرَّبَا قُرْبَانًا فَتُقُبِّلَ مِن أَحَدِهِمَا وَلَمْ يُتَقَبَّلْ مِنَ الآخَرِ قَالَ لَأَقْتُلَنَّكَ قَالَ إِنَّمَا يَتَقَبَّلُ اللهُ مِنَ الْمُتَّقِينَ {المائدة/27}

One of the brothers in the above mentioned ayah can have the negative attitudes, negative criticism and fault-finding attitude due to the absence of taqwa. The other one can have the positive and constructive attitude sourced from taqwa. Yet, Allah ﷻ accepts the works, actions and all the efforts from the ones who have taqwa as mentioned قَالَ إِنَّمَا يَتَقَبَّلُ اللهُ مِنَ الْمُتَّقِينَ {المائدة/27}.

May Allah ﷻ give us taqwa and accept our amal and works with the Divine Fadl, Grace and Karam, Amìn.

Therefore, one should make the utmost effort to be with the people of taqwa in the works of the dìn so that their efforts and amal can be accepted by Allah ﷻ, inshAllah.

On the other hand, we should try to avoid ourselves judging others and having su-i zann, bad thoughts, about others for the absence or lack of taqwa.

External taqwa is the following sunnah of Rasulullah ﷺ in fiqh rulings as outlined by the Qurãn and Hadith of Rasulullah ﷺ.

Internal taqwa is the purification of the heart with tawhid, with absence of all types of shirk, absence of riya, kibir, arrogance, jealousy, hasad and other deadly diseases.

Looking a person externally for the existence of taqwa, and assuming the internal existence of taqwa can be a mistake.

Looking a person externally for the absence of taqwa and assuming the internal absence can also be a mistake.

May Allah ﷻ guide us to be with the people of taqwa, Amìn.

Yet, one should remember that Allah ﷻ can give barakah and acceptance for the people of taqwa.

One of the signs of people of taqwa is that when a person is with them, they can remember Allah ﷻ and Rasulullah ﷺ.

The spin system, as mentioned in particle physics, of the heart, mind and all the spiritual faculties tend to align in their intrinsic position

---

152. [Allah] said, "Then indeed, it is forbidden to them for forty years [in which] they will wander throughout the land. So do not grieve over the defiantly disobedient people." And recite to them the story of Adam's two sons, in truth, when they both offered a sacrifice [to Allah], and it was accepted from one of them but was not accepted from the other. Said [the latter], "I will surely kill you." Said [the former], "Indeed, Allah only accepts from the righteous [who fear Him].

towards Allah ﷻ due to this invisible magnetic field of taqwa in the medium.

May Allah ﷻ makes us from the people of taqwa, Amin.

<h2 style="text-align:center">Juz 23</h2>

Sûrah 36 Yā-sìn

[66-67]

Understanding the Ni'mahs of Allah ﷻ through its Opposite

وَلَوْ نَشَاءُ لَطَمَسْنَا عَلَى أَعْيُنِهِمْ فَاسْتَبَقُوا الصِّرَاطَ فَأَنَّى يُبْصِرُونَ {يس/66} 153 وَلَوْ نَشَاءُ لَمَسَخْنَاهُمْ عَلَى مَكَانَتِهِمْ فَمَا اسْتَطَاعُوا مُضِيًّا وَلَا يَرْجِعُونَ {يس/67}

One can analyze the above ayahs and below ayahs as

أَفَرَأَيْتُم مَّا تَحْرُثُونَ {الواقعة/63} 154 أَأَنتُمْ تَزْرَعُونَهُ أَمْ نَحْنُ الزَّارِعُونَ {الواقعة/64} لَوْ نَشَاءُ لَجَعَلْنَاهُ حُطَامًا فَظَلْتُمْ تَفَكَّهُونَ {الواقعة/65} إِنَّا لَمُغْرَمُونَ {الواقعة/66} بَلْ نَحْنُ مَحْرُومُونَ {الواقعة/67} أَفَرَأَيْتُمُ الْمَاءَ الَّذِي تَشْرَبُونَ {الواقعة/68} أَأَنتُمْ أَنزَلْتُمُوهُ مِنَ الْمُزْنِ أَمْ نَحْنُ الْمُنزِلُونَ {الواقعة/69} لَوْ نَشَاءُ جَعَلْنَاهُ أُجَاجًا فَلَوْلَا تَشْكُرُونَ {الواقعة/70}

In both sets of the ayahs in Sûrah Yāsìn and Sûrah al-Waqia'h, there is the expression وَلَوْ نَشَاءُ. Allah ﷻ mentions us this expression for us to understand, realize and appreciate countless ni'mahs of Allah ﷻ.

Sometimes and most of the time, we take things granted. Yet, thinking and realizing the possibility of the absence of these ni'mahs can really make the person come into the reality from the unreal pampered ballooned states of arrogance in the ego, self or nafs.

When a person sees a blind person, he or she appreciates what they have better in our eyesights. When a person sees a bed-ridden, disabled, crippled or spastic person, we tend to appreciate what we have in our

---

153. And if We willed, We could have obliterated their eyes, and they would race to [find] the path, and how could they see? And if We willed, We could have deformed them, [paralyzing them] in their places so they would not be able to proceed, nor could they return.

154. And have you seen that [seed] which you sow? Is it you who makes it grow, or are We the grower? If We willed, We could make it [dry] debris, and you would remain in wonder, [Saying], "Indeed, we are [now] in debt; Rather, we have been deprived." And have you seen the water that you drink? Is it you who brought it down from the clouds, or is it We who bring it down? If We willed, We could make it bitter, so why are you not grateful?

bodies. When there is no rain or acid-rain, people appreciate rain that Allah ﷻ constantly sends us, SubhanAllah.

SubhanAllah, we are constantly in constant gaflah and do not realize all these endless ni'mahs of Allah ﷻ to be grateful, thankful and appreciative as mentioned {الواقعة/70} فَلَوْ لَا تَشْكُرُونَ

May Allah ﷻ makes us from the Shakirûn, Amìn.

Juz 25

Sûrah 43-al-Zukhruf

[52]

The Realities of Ana (I)

أَمْ أَنَا خَيْرٌ مِّنْ هَذَا الَّذِي هُوَ مَهِينٌ وَلَا يَكَادُ يُبِينُ {الزخرف/52}[155]

When we analyze the expression أَنَا خَيْرٌ مِّنْ in the above ayah, one can realize other similar usage of this expression in other parts of the Qurān as[156]

قَالَ مَا مَنَعَكَ أَلَّا تَسْجُدَ إِذْ أَمَرْتُكَ قَالَ أَنَا خَيْرٌ مِّنْهُ خَلَقْتَنِي مِن نَّارٍ وَخَلَقْتَهُ مِن طِينٍ {الأعراف/12}

قَالَ أَنَا خَيْرٌ مِّنْهُ خَلَقْتَنِي مِن نَّارٍ وَخَلَقْتَهُ مِن طِينٍ {ص/76}[157]

One should realize our own ana as mentioned with أَنَا. In the human and Jinn realities of أَنَا, when there is a free will with choice and a given degree of freedom of movability by Allah ﷻ, then the reality of أَنَا tend to compare everything with itself called ana or I or أَنَا.

In this comparison of أَنَا, all the comparability come around أَنَا and others. According to some, ana is given to us to compare ourselves with other beings to reach to Allah ﷻ with humbleness and humility.

The raw state of nafs is classified in terminology as nafs-ammara or raw nafs or raw ego.

---

155. Or am I [not] better than this one who is insignificant and hardly makes himself clear?
156. [Allah] said, "What prevented you from prostrating when I commanded you?" [Satan] said, "I am better than him. You created me from fire and created him from clay."
157. He said, "I am better than him. You created me from fire and created him from clay."

In this reality of أَنَا, ana or أَنَا in its raw state, it always assumes that is always better, higher, greater, and superior than others.

In this assumption and approach of أَنَا, the person wants the other or others all destroyed, fail, lose and to be in pain to prove that his or her أَنَا is better.

In this sense, a person's أَنَا can desire to see others to suffer, to lose and to fail. A group أَنَا embedded with the same perspective can desire to see other groups to suffer, to lose and to fail.

Yet, if this is the reality, then what should one do?

Allah ﷻ has given us mind and emotions.

First, it is critical to force ourselves to even imitate to throw the idea inside our أَنَا as "what if the other person's struggle is better than yours? What if Allah ﷻ accepts his or her effort and but not accept yours?"

This is mentioned as[158] وَاتْلُ عَلَيْهِمْ نَبَأَ ابْنَيْ آدَمَ بِالْحَقِّ إِذْ قَرَّبَا قُرْبَانًا فَتُقُبِّلَ مِن أَحَدِهِمَا وَلَمْ يُتَقَبَّلْ مِنَ الآخَرِ قَالَ لَأَقْتُلَنَّكَ قَالَ إِنَّمَا يَتَقَبَّلُ اللّهُ مِنَ الْمُتَّقِينَ {المائدة/27}

At this state a nafs surrounded with invasion of raw ana with this feelings of أَنَا خَيْرٌ مِّنْ هَذَا, can have two possible positions. One ana can journey or sail in the shores of imān.

Choice of Iman

The first position is the position of a believer. When they are reminded about the reality of "If Allah ﷻ accepts the other person's effort but not yours", then immediately the person can be in the invasion of imān mixed with invasion of raw ana with these feelings of أَنَا خَيْرٌ مِّنْ هَذَا.

This is a very critical state for the person now to lose or to gain the battle against the raw ana who claims أَنَا خَيْرٌ مِّنْ هَذَا.

If the person continues through his free-will mindful and logical engagements in his inner self in the fist fight against his or her raw-ana, he or she may find oneself in the mixed phase of imān pulling the person for istigfar, tawba, refuge from the temptations of nafs and Shaytān. This can be indicated as[159] وَإِمَّا يَنزَغَنَّكَ مِنَ الشَّيْطَانِ نَزْغٌ فَاسْتَعِذْ بِاللهِ

---

158. And recite to them the story of Adam's two sons, in truth, when they both offered a sacrifice [to Allah], and it was accepted from one of them but was not accepted from the other. Said [the latter], "I will surely kill you." Said [the former], "Indeed, Allah only accepts from the righteous [who fear Him].

159. And if an evil suggestion comes to you from Satan, then seek refuge in Allah. Indeed, He is Hearing and Knowing. Indeed, those who fear Allah - when an impulse touches them from Satan, they remember [Him] and at once they have insight.

إِنَّهُ سَمِيعٌ عَلِيمٌ {الأعراف/200} إِنَّ الَّذِينَ اتَّقَواْ إِذَا مَسَّهُمْ طَائِفٌ مِّنَ الشَّيْطَانِ تَذَكَّرُواْ فَإِذَا هُم مُّبْصِرُونَ {الأعراف/102}

On the other hand, the person can feel at this state the disgusting feelings with the pamperings of raw ana and Shaytān as indicated with أَنَا خَيْرٌ مِّنْ هَذَا.

Ice to Liquid State

This can be similar to phase diagram of water coming from solid state to liquid state as

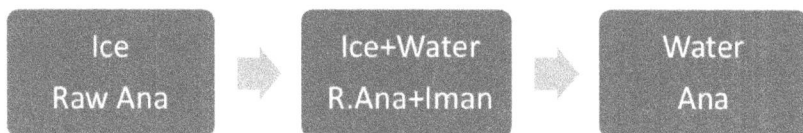

As one remembers from physics and chemistry, the phase change is represented in the mixed of ice and water. Raw ana as أَنَا خَيْرٌ مِّنْ هَذَا can be similar to the solid state of ice. The mental initiated struggle with imān with the teachings of the Qurān and sunnah against the temptations of raw ana and Shaytān can be similar to the mixed state of ice and water.

It needs a lot of energy to move from this mixed of ice-water into water. Similarly, when the person makes the intention of struggle with the humbleness and humility making their inclination towards imān, then the transformational energy can be given by Allah ﷻ with the Fadl, Karam, Grace, and Rahmah of Allah ﷻ. This can be called in terminology as guidance or Hidayah.

Liquid Water State -Nafs Lawwamah

Then, the next level of ana is similar to the liquid state water which can be called ana or nafs lawwamah. The nafs constantly struggles.

This is the position and victory of iman. When the person embodies the reality of the constant struggle against nafs and Shaytān sometimes winning and sometimes losing, then this is a higher state than the raw ana, nafs-ammarah. This state is called embodiment of struggle, nafs-lawwamah. This is why a person who has a free will deems to attract the Fadl, Karam and Rahmah of Allah ﷻ because they are in the embodiment of struggle against their raw ana in order not to continue in this raw state of أَنَا خَيْرٌ مِّنْ هَذَا, and try to embody the state of imān with humbleness, humility and submission and appreciation for the choices of Allah ﷻ. A person of imān does not care in reality who is better than others, but always looks forward in the intrinsic and struggles to please Allah ﷻ.

The liquid state of water can represent this constant fluidity of struggle for the person against the raw ana. Yet, this initial intention of struggle and later embodied state of struggle of imān can be the mystery of guidance and Hidayah from Allah ﷻ with the Fadl, Karam, Grace and Rahmah of Allah ﷻ as a virtuous state as mentioned[160] وَالَّذِينَ جَاهَدُوا فِينَا لَنَهْدِيَنَّهُمْ سُبُلَنَا وَإِنَّ اللَّهَ لَمَعَ الْمُحْسِنِينَ {العنكبوت/69}.

This embodiment can take the person to the higher maqams and stations with the Fadl and Grace of Allah ﷻ.

Liquid to Gas State

This ana in the liquid state embodied the liquidity of struggle at the stations of nafs-lawwamah can have the potentials of going higher similar to liquid water state transforming into gas state of vapor.

In this state, water is not contained but can evaporate. The movability or degrees of freedom of the water molecules have more freedom, hurriyah. This can be similar to nafs-mutmainna. In this state, the person is pleased with everything with imān, taslīm, tawakkul and itminān.

In this regard, the real freedom and movability is the movability of the rūh in one's attachment to Allah ﷻ being unshackled from the solid state of iced ana claiming constantly with raw ana with the feelings of أَنَا خَيْرٌ مِّنْ هَذَا.

One can observe a similar diagram from liquid state to gas state which takes energy and further effort. Similarly, it takes further effort, istiqamah, and struggle to reach to the levels of nafs mutmainna and ihsan with the higher movability of not being attached to anything but increased attachment to Allah ﷻ. The more the person embodies La ilaha illa Allah, the more the person becomes free and less attached to the chained shackles of this dunya.

---

160. And those who strive for Us - We will surely guide them to Our ways. And indeed, Allah is with the doers of good.

The more the person gets unshackled from these chains the higher states can be as mentioned[161] يَا أَيَّتُهَا النَّفْسُ الْمُطْمَئِنَّةُ {27/الفجر} ارْجِعِي إِلَى رَبِّكِ رَاضِيَةً مَّرْضِيَّةً {28/الفجر} فَادْخُلِي فِي عِبَادِي {29/الفجر} وَادْخُلِي جَنَّتِي {30/الفجر}

The states of nafs-mutmainna can go further states with full unshacklement by the embodiment of fully turning to Allah ﷻ as mentioned يَا أَيَّتُهَا النَّفْسُ الْمُطْمَئِنَّةُ {27/الفجر} ارْجِعِي إِلَى رَبِّكِ.

This higher state can be similar to the plasma state that are observed in stars or in fluorescent light. The plasma state generally considered a combined or mixed state similar to the states of رَاضِيَةً مَّرْضِيَّةً. Mufassirun and tasawwfifun had a discussion whose rida comes first as "when the a'bd is pleased with Allah ﷻ, then Allah ﷻ is pleased with the person. Or, when Allah ﷻ is pleased with the person, then the a'bd is pleased with Allah ﷻ." Yet, this combined state of 'abd and Ma'bud or mahluq or Khaliq relationship can be SubhanAllah very described as رَاضِيَةً مَّرْضِيَّةً.

This real and ideal state of the person is very high similar to the stars in the universe with the plasma state. This state of رَاضِيَةً مَّرْضِيَّةً can be the state of muqarribun, the real ones who are at the highest level with Allah ﷻ as mentioned[162] فَادْخُلِي فِي عِبَادِي {29/الفجر}

Now, this is the real Jannah and real happiness as mentioned[163] وَادْخُلِي جَنَّتِي {30/الفجر}.

Allahumma Ja'alna min al Muwahiddin wal maqurrabun ma'K wa ma'a Rasuluna wa Imamana Muhammad ﷺ Amìn.

Solid Ice State

When we look at the other possibility that the ana who has the claims and feelings of أَنَا خَيْرٌ مِّنْ هَذَا, is reminded with the realities of imān about the reality of fallacy of their own raw ana, then he or she does take any heed but he or she increases their solid attachment with the raw ana of أَنَا خَيْرٌ مِّنْ هَذَا, and gets aggravated and get crazy in order to prove their fallacy.

One get realize this aggravation in all of the below statements in similar raw ana cases but with different players at different times and contexts.

---

161. Return to your Lord, well-pleased and pleasing [to Him], And enter among My [righteous] servants And enter My Paradise."
162. And enter among My [righteous] servants
163. And enter My Paradise."

When Allah ﷻ reminds Iblis the reality as[164] قَالَ يَا إِبْلِيسُ مَا مَنَعَكَ أَن تَسْجُدَ لِمَا خَلَقْتُ بِيَدَيَّ أَسْتَكْبَرْتَ أَمْ كُنتَ مِنَ الْعَالِينَ {ص/57}, then he gets aggravated in front of Rabbul Alamin without any adab as mentioned[165] قَالَ فَبِعِزَّتِكَ لَأُغْوِيَنَّهُمْ أَجْمَعِينَ {ص/828} إِلَّا عِبَادَكَ مِنْهُمُ الْمُخْلَصِينَ {ص/83}.

When Musa as reminds Firawn the realities of iman as[166] قَالَ رَبُّ السَّمَاوَاتِ وَالْأَرْضِ وَمَا بَيْنَهُمَا إِن كُنتُم مُّوقِنِينَ {الشعراء/24} قَالَ لِمَنْ حَوْلَهُ أَلَا تَسْتَمِعُونَ {الشعراء/25} قَالَ رَبُّكُمْ وَرَبُّ آبَائِكُمُ الْأَوَّلِينَ {الشعراء/26} قَالَ إِنَّ رَسُولَكُمُ الَّذِي أُرْسِلَ إِلَيْكُمْ لَمَجْنُونٌ {الشعراء/27} قَالَ رَبُّ الْمَشْرِقِ وَالْمَغْرِبِ وَمَا بَيْنَهُمَا إِن كُنتُمْ تَعْقِلُونَ {الشعراء/28} then, Firawn gets aggravated as mentioned[167] قَالَ لَئِنِ اتَّخَذْتَ إِلَٰهًا غَيْرِي لَأَجْعَلَنَّكَ مِنَ الْمَسْجُونِينَ {الشعراء/29}.

When even Firawn sees the realities of iman with obvious signs of miracles, he gets further aggravated as mentioned[168] فَأَلْقَى مُوسَى عَصَاهُ فَإِذَا هِيَ تَلْقَفُ مَا يَأْفِكُونَ {الشعراء/45} فَأُلْقِيَ السَّحَرَةُ سَاجِدِينَ {الشعراء/46} قَالُوا آمَنَّا بِرَبِّ الْعَالَمِينَ {الشعراء/47} رَبِّ مُوسَى وَهَارُونَ {الشعراء/48} قَالَ آمَنتُمْ لَهُ قَبْلَ أَنْ آذَنَ لَكُمْ إِنَّهُ لَكَبِيرُكُمُ الَّذِي عَلَّمَكُمُ السِّحْرَ فَلَسَوْفَ تَعْلَمُونَ لَأُقَطِّعَنَّ أَيْدِيَكُمْ وَأَرْجُلَكُم مِّنْ خِلَافٍ وَلَأُصَلِّبَنَّكُمْ أَجْمَعِينَ {الشعراء/49}.

When of the brothers with iman remind the other brother realities of iman as وَاتْلُ عَلَيْهِمْ نَبَأَ ابْنَيْ آدَمَ بِالْحَقِّ إِذْ قَرَّبَا قُرْبَانًا فَتُقُبِّلَ مِن أَحَدِهِمَا وَلَمْ يُتَقَبَّلْ مِنَ الْآخَرِ قَالَ لَأَقْتُلَنَّكَ قَالَ إِنَّمَا يَتَقَبَّلُ اللَّهُ مِنَ الْمُتَّقِينَ {المائدة/27}[169] لَئِن بَسَطتَ إِلَيَّ يَدَكَ لِتَقْتُلَنِي مَا أَنَا بِبَاسِطٍ يَدِيَ إِلَيْكَ لِأَقْتُلَكَ إِنِّي أَخَافُ اللَّهَ رَبَّ الْعَالَمِينَ {المائدة/28}[170] إِنِّي أُرِيدُ أَن تَبُوءَ

---

164. [Allah] said, "O Iblees, what prevented you from prostrating to that which I created with My hands? Were you arrogant [then], or were you [already] among the haughty?"

165. [Iblees] said, "By your might, I will surely mislead them all Except, among them, Your chosen servants."

166. [Moses] said, "The Lord of the heavens and earth and that between them, if you should be convinced." [Pharaoh] said to those around him, "Do you not hear?" [Moses] said, "Your Lord and the Lord of your first forefathers." [Pharaoh] said, "Indeed, your 'messenger' who has been sent to you is mad." [Moses] said, "Lord of the east and the west and that between them, if you were to reason."

167. [Pharaoh] said, "If you take a god other than me, I will surely place you among those imprisoned."

168. Then Moses threw his staff, and at once it devoured what they falsified. So the magicians fell down in prostration [to Allah]. They said, "We have believed in the Lord of the worlds, The Lord of Moses and Aaron." [Pharaoh] said, "You believed Moses before I gave you permission. Indeed, he is your leader who has taught you magic, but you are going to know. I will surely cut off your hands and your feet on opposite sides, and I will surely crucify you all."

169. And recite to them the story of Adam's two sons, in truth, when they both offered a sacrifice [to Allah], and it was accepted from one of them but was not accepted from the other. Said [the latter], "I will surely kill you." Said [the former], "Indeed, Allah only accepts from the righteous [who fear Him].

170. If you should raise your hand against me to kill me - I shall not raise my hand against you to kill you. Indeed, I fear Allah, Lord of the worlds. Indeed I want you to obtain [thereby] my sin and your sin so you will be among the companions of the Fire. And that is the recompense of wrongdoers."

ثُمَّ، بِإِثْمِي وَإِثْمِكَ فَتَكُونَ مِنْ أَصْحَابِ النَّارِ وَذَلِكَ جَزَاءُ الظَّالِمِينَ {المائدة/29}then, the other
brother gets aggravated and kills his brother as mentioned[171] فَطَوَّعَتْ لَهُ
نَفْسُهُ قَتْلَ أَخِيهِ فَقَتَلَهُ فَأَصْبَحَ مِنَ الْخَاسِرِينَ {المائدة/30}.

This is the position of kufr. This is why a person who has a free will
deems to be punished because they wanted to continue in this raw state
of أَنَا خَيْرٌ مِّنْ هَذَا, and embody this state of kufr.

May Allah ﷻ protect us from kufr, Amìn.

Love: Exclusivity or Inclusivity

One should consider if a person wants exclusivity or inclusivity if a
person claims to love Allah ﷻ with imān.

The real imān and love of Allah ﷻ requires not exclusivity only for
themselves or their own ego but they desire inclusivity as for others Allah
ﷻ and love Allah ﷻ. They try to embody that the Fadl and Rahmah of
Allah ﷻ is so vast and other fellows can also try to please Allah ﷻ and be
better in this struggle than this person.

This type of exclusivity, only desiring the love and the pleasure of
Allah ﷻ for only oneself, can indicate another deep sickness as indicated
by raw ana of the state أَنَا خَيْرٌ مِّنْ هَذَا.

Yes, one can understand sometimes love requires jealousy and not
sharing the loved with anyone. This is a reality and can be virtuous level
if the person knows how to use it in oneself especially when a person
only embodies tawhid and La ilaha illa Allah ﷻ.

Allah ﷻ is al-Ghayur. There is no one who deserves to be loved
except Allah ﷻ. Therefore, the person in this absolute reality and truth
should only turn to Allah and please Allah ﷻ with tawhid, La ilaha illa
Allah.

If otherwise, if the person turns other things, this is called shirk.

This reality of La ilaha illa Allah, tawhid is not for just this ana or for
this person, but all the people. Then, this absolute reality requires that
everyone should turn to Allah ﷻ with imān.

One should not sometimes mix this with the terms such as sharing
as human realms of limited language require words suitable to their
limited beings.

---

171. And his soul permitted to him the murder of his brother, so he killed him and became
among the losers.

Allah ﷻ is the M'abud, Khaliq, and Rabb of everything and everyone. This is the reality. Desiring everyone to realize this absolute reality is another reality.

If a person loves someone and another person hates, or use a bad language or hurtful engagement about the beloved, then the person, the lover can get hurt as well. Then, the real lover can go to the hater in an hurt way and say why do hurt me by talking against the one I love and using a hate, bad and hurtful language.

Below ayahs can make the person relate this reality as[172] إِنَّ الَّذِينَ يُؤْذُونَ اللَّهَ وَرَسُولَهُ لَعَنَهُمُ اللَّهُ فِي الدُّنْيَا وَالْآخِرَةِ وَأَعَدَّ لَهُمْ عَذَابًا مُهِينًا {الأحزاب/57} وَالَّذِينَ يُؤْذُونَ الْمُؤْمِنِينَ وَالْمُؤْمِنَاتِ بِغَيْرِ مَا اكْتَسَبُوا فَقَدِ احْتَمَلُوا بُهْتَانًا وَإِثْمًا مُبِينًا {الأحزاب/58}. The ayah can indicate the real believers of iman are hurt due to the ones hurtful language and attitudes towards the Beloved and the beloved one, Allah ﷻ and Rasulullah ﷺ.

If a person loves someone, if others like and love someone, can a person say "only I can love that person but no one else?"

Love is a general term.

If the beloved is one's wife, then there is an intimate relationship with the husband and wife. Therefore, it is encouraged to say "that is my wife, I do not want anyone to look at her with a feelings of gender relationships." This is the feelings of ghayur of a husband as mentioned in the hadith [3][173].

Yet, a genuine husband will be hurt if a person hurts the feelings of his wife and encourage animosity for his wife. One can remember the case of Rasulullah ﷺ, he ﷺ did not want to attend a dinner invitation when ummahatul mumin, Aisha (ranha) was not invited [4][174]. Rasulullah ﷺ did not attend the dinner until she (ranha) was also invited.

If the beloved is a father, then one can think a son's relationship with his father. Is it ok to claim and say "I want my dad only to love me but not my other brothers,"?

Yet, one should realize that this is not real. A father is father for all children. When a son claims only exclusive love for himself, but

---

172. Indeed, those who abuse Allah and His Messenger - Allah has cursed them in this world and the Hereafter and prepared for them a humiliating punishment. And those who harm believing men and believing women for [something] other than what they have earned have certainly born upon themselves a slander and manifest sin.
173. Hadith # 97/44
174. Hadith #2037

excluding the others, then this can show a disease of the heart as not sharing, selfish, arrogant state of أَنَا خَيْرٌ مِّنْ هَذَا. In this case, the real embodiment of love requires for the person to desire that all the sons to love and respect their father and follow his commands. Especially, if the son knows that he will attract pleasure and love of his father more when he embodies this attitude then, he can be more encouraged. One can view this dynamic of diseased hearts hiding behind love in the entire Sûrah Yûsuf in father and son relationships.

If the beloved is Rasulullah ﷺ, then his position ﷺ is at a higher levl than a father for us. Loving Rasulullah is the essence and part of our imân. Desiring others to love him is reality because he ﷺ was to sent all the creation by Allah ﷻ.

Rasulullah ﷺ is like father of all and the mothers, ummahatul mumin, is our mothers and mothers for all people. The love of Rasulullah ﷺ, the love of ahlu-bayt, the love of things what Rasulullah ﷺ loved becomes natural and obligatory for us. Then, reminding people this reality who has hate, distance, and isolation from their real father Rasulullah ﷺ becomes obligatory and a natural responsibility for us. When a person sees a child, who has been distanced from his father for many years, and one day, one can witness a child meeting his father. Any genuine person will be happy and crying at this scene. Similarly, people today are separated from Rasulullah ﷺ. People are born as orphans at homes without knowing Rasulullah ﷺ.

If the beloved is Allah ﷻ, Who is the Creator, Khaliq, Ma'bud and Rabb of the person. Loving Allah ﷻ is essence. Desiring others to love Allah ﷻ is reality because Allah ﷻ is the Creator, Khaliq, and Rabb of all the creation.

Desiring to love what Allah ﷻ loves such as Rasulullah ﷺ, all other prophets, Sahabah, the Qurân, ummahatul mumin, ahlulullah, angels, Jibril as Mikail as and all others become natural and obligatory for us. Then, reminding people about this reality who has hate, distance, and isolation from their Creator, Khaliq, and Rabb ﷻ become obligatory and natural-fitri disposition for our iman. When a person witnesses another person who has been wandering around, distanced and isolated from his or her Creator, Khaliq, Rabb ﷻ, for many years, and one day witnesses that this lost person realizes and connects his or her Creator, Khaliq, Rabb ﷻ.

Any genuine person will be happy and crying at this scene. Similarly, people today are separated from Allah ﷻ People are born at homes without knowing Allah ﷻ. One can remember the case of Balqis and this scene in Sûrah Naml, SubhanAllah.

Allah ﷻ mentions for many years she was a lost wanderer as mentioned[175]

إِنِّي وَجَدتُّ امْرَأَةً تَمْلِكُهُمْ وَأُوتِيَتْ مِن كُلِّ شَيْءٍ وَلَهَا عَرْشٌ عَظِيمٌ {النمل/23} وَجَدتُّهَا وَقَوْمَهَا يَسْجُدُونَ لِلشَّمْسِ مِن دُونِ اللَّهِ وَزَيَّنَ لَهُمُ الشَّيْطَانُ أَعْمَالَهُمْ فَصَدَّهُمْ عَنِ السَّبِيلِ فَهُمْ لَا يَهْتَدُونَ {النمل/24}

وَصَدَّهَا مَا كَانَت تَّعْبُدُ مِن دُونِ اللَّهِ إِنَّهَا كَانَتْ مِن قَوْمٍ كَافِرِينَ {النمل/43}[176]

After many years of as a lost wanderer, Allah ﷻ depicts this moment of realizing and finding Allah ﷻ as her real Rabb as mentioned[177] قَالَتْ رَبِّ إِنِّي ظَلَمْتُ نَفْسِي وَأَسْلَمْتُ مَعَ سُلَيْمَانَ لِلَّهِ رَبِّ الْعَالَمِينَ {النمل/44}

Therefore, we should try to embody the dua of Rasulullah ﷺ as

اللَّهُمَّ إِنِّي أَسْأَلُكَ حُبَّكَ وَحُبَّ مَنْ يُحِبُّكَ وَالْعَمَلَ الَّذِي يُبَلِّغُنِي حُبَّكَ اللَّهُمَّ اجْعَلْ حُبَّكَ أَحَبَّ إِلَىَّ مِنْ نَفْسِي وَأَهْلِي وَمِنَ الْمَاءِ الْبَارِدِ

[4] (hadith#3490).

Our genuine imān of La ilaha illa Allah Muhammadun Rasulullah require the love of Allah ﷻ and Rasulullah ﷺ. This love of Allah ﷻ and Rasulullah ﷺ requires to bring the people back who are lost, distanced from the Beloved and beloved. Allah ﷻ is our Rabb and Khaliq. Rasulullah ﷺ is our father that people are looking for advice and guidance.

May Allah ﷻ make us love Allah ﷻ and Rasulullah ﷺ with true imān and ikhlās, Amìn.

---

175. Indeed, I found [there] a woman ruling them, and she has been given of all things, and she has a great throne. I found her and her people prostrating to the sun instead of Allah, and Satan has made their deeds pleasing to them and averted them from [His] way, so they are not guided,

176. And that which she was worshipping other than Allah had averted her [from submission to Him]. Indeed, she was from a disbelieving people."

177. She was told, "Enter the palace." But when she saw it, she thought it was a body of water and uncovered her shins [to wade through]. He said, "Indeed, it is a palace [whose floor is] made smooth with glass." She said, "My Lord, indeed I have wronged myself, and I submit with Solomon to Allah, Lord of the worlds."

May Allah ﷻ makes us love what Allah ﷻ loves and make us don't love what Allah ﷻ does not love.

May Allah ﷻ make us bring people back to Allah ﷻ and Rasulullah ﷺ who are lost wanderers and looking for their Rabb and Rasulullah ﷺ for guidance, Amìn.

Allahumma salli ala sayyidina Muhammad, alfu alfu marrah.

Constant Struggle with Mind & Intellect with Free Will

وَإِمَّا يَنزَغَنَّكَ مِنَ الشَّيْطَانِ نَزْغٌ فَاسْتَعِذْ بِاللهِ إِنَّهُ سَمِيعٌ عَلِيمٌ {الأعراف/200}[178]

وَإِمَّا يَنزَغَنَّكَ مِنَ الشَّيْطَانِ نَزْغٌ فَاسْتَعِذْ بِاللهِ إِنَّهُ هُوَ السَّمِيعُ الْعَلِيمُ {فصلت/36}[179]

One should remember that as long as the person is alive, he or she is not safe from the poisonous arrows of Shaytān pampering and activating the nafs-ammarah.

One should always follow the guidelines of the Qurān and Sunnah of Rasulullah ﷺ in all matters.

Especially, when the things get blurry for the person due to attacks of Shaytān and pampering of the nafs-ammarah, it is very critical at this time and at all times to push oneself mentally and intellectually to use one's free will and choice under the guidelines of the Qurān and Sunnah of Rasulullah ﷺ. At the same time, taking refuge in Allah ﷻ without any hawl and quwwah and not trusting one's own free will is the key.

When we look at and review the usûl of mutassawifîn, this is the methodology that they have generally followed.

For example, when a person who has some knowledge receives some feelings of hasad, arrogance and disapproval about the knowledge of another person who may be consider a scholar or a'lìm, then the free-will of this person necessitates to remind oneself mentally and intellectually the dangers of hasad, arrogance and superiority under the guidance of the Qurān and Sunnah of Rasulullah ﷺ.

During all these mental and logical reminders, one should constantly refuge in Allah ﷻ as mentioned وَإِمَّا يَنزَغَنَّكَ مِنَ الشَّيْطَانِ نَزْغٌ فَاسْتَعِذْ بِاللهِ, proclaiming one's insufficiency of handling this case mentally by

---

178. And if an evil suggestion comes to you from Satan, then seek refuge in Allah. Indeed, He is Hearing and Knowing.
179. And if there comes to you from Satan an evil suggestion, then seek refuge in Allah. Indeed, He is the Hearing, the Knowing.

one's free will but handling and overcoming it with the istia'za-refuge in Allah ﷻ.

This is a reality.

There is no position of security and safety in our relationship with Allah ﷻ until we die and the period of tests and trials due to the acquisition of free-will are over.

As the person can go forward in religious affairs, the types of intrinsic tests and trials pampered by Shaytān activating the nafs-ammarah can become more convoluted and complex.

Yet, in all these, one's inner and outer disposition of the person require وَإِمَّا يَنزَغَنَّكَ مِنَ الشَّيْطَانِ نَزْغٌ فَاسْتَعِذْ بِاللهِ along with mental and intellectual engagement of the free-will to counter-argue against the pampering of Shaytān.

These cases can be vivid in the Qurãn as[180]

قَالَ لَقَدْ ظَلَمَكَ بِسُؤَالِ نَعْجَتِكَ إِلَى نِعَاجِهِ وَإِنَّ كَثِيرًا مِّنَ الْخُلَطَاءِ لَيَبْغِي بَعْضُهُمْ عَلَى بَعْضٍ إِلَّا الَّذِينَ آمَنُوا وَعَمِلُوا الصَّالِحَاتِ وَقَلِيلٌ مَّا هُمْ وَظَنَّ دَاوُودُ أَنَّمَا فَتَنَّاهُ فَاسْتَغْفَرَ رَبَّهُ وَخَرَّ رَاكِعًا وَأَنَابَ (سجدة مستحبة)﴿ص/24﴾ فَغَفَرْنَا لَهُ ذَلِكَ وَإِنَّ لَهُ عِندَنَا لَزُلْفَى وَحُسْنَ مَآبٍ ﴿ص/25﴾ وَلَقَدْ فَتَنَّا سُلَيْمَانَ وَأَلْقَيْنَا عَلَى كُرْسِيِّهِ جَسَدًا ثُمَّ أَنَابَ ﴿ص/34﴾[181] قَالَ رَبِّ اغْفِرْ لِي وَهَبْ لِي مُلْكًا لَّا يَنبَغِي لِأَحَدٍ مِّنْ بَعْدِي إِنَّكَ أَنتَ الْوَهَّابُ ﴿ص/35﴾

Here are the two prophets of Allah ﷻ, Dawûd as and Sulaymãn as.

The first case indicates وَلَقَدْ وَظَنَّ دَاوُودُ أَنَّمَا فَتَنَّاهُ. The second indicates فَتَنَّا سُلَيْمَانَ.

Yet in both cases, the people of Allah ﷻ take the positions of

- ▶ فَاسْتَغْفَرَ رَبَّهُ
- ▶ وَخَرَّ رَاكِعًا وَأَنَابَ
- ▶ ثُمَّ أَنَابَ
- ▶ رَبِّ اغْفِرْ لِي

---

180. [David] said, "He has certainly wronged you in demanding your ewe [in addition] to his ewes. And indeed, many associates oppress one another, except for those who believe and do righteous deeds - and few are they." And David became certain that We had tried him, and he asked forgiveness of his Lord and fell down bowing [in prostration] and turned in repentance [to Allah]. So We forgave him that; and indeed, for him is nearness to Us and a good place of return.

181. And We certainly tried Solomon and placed on his throne a body; then he returned. He said, "My Lord, forgive me and grant me a kingdom such as will not belong to anyone after me. Indeed, You are the Bestower."

The above expression can indicate constant inābah-turning to Allah ﷻ with istighfār and istiā'za-taking refuge in Allah ﷻ.

One can realize this reality of insecurity in one's relationship with Allah ﷻ until one dies as mentioned in the statement of Yusuf as[182] رَبِّ قَدْ آتَيْتَنِي مِنَ الْمُلْكِ وَعَلَّمْتَنِي مِن تَأْوِيلِ الْأَحَادِيثِ فَاطِرَ السَّمَاوَاتِ وَالْأَرْضِ أَنتَ وَلِيِّي فِي الدُّنْيَا وَالآخِرَةِ تَوَفَّنِي مُسْلِمًا وَأَلْحِقْنِي بِالصَّالِحِينَ {يوسف/101}

The statement of Yusuf as تَوَفَّنِي مُسْلِمًا وَأَلْحِقْنِي بِالصَّالِحِينَ can indicate this reality of constant refuge with istigfar and tawbah, inābah and awbah to Allah ﷻ. Yet, the person is not safe that at any point until one dies, he or she lose the trial. This is the reality as mentioned by Yusuf as.

Allahumma Salli A'lā Sayyidinā Muhammad.

Allahumma La Takilni Nafsan Tarfata A'yn.

Allahumma Ja'alna min attawabìn, Amìn. Allahumma Salli wa Barik a'lā Sayyidinā wa Habibinā Muhammad ﷺ.

Case of Angels and Other Beings Commenting the Realities with Their Knowledge without the Effect of Shaytān

وَإِذْ قَالَ رَبُّكَ لِلْمَلَائِكَةِ إِنِّي جَاعِلٌ فِي الْأَرْضِ خَلِيفَةً قَالُواْ أَتَجْعَلُ فِيهَا مَن يُفْسِدُ فِيهَا وَيَسْفِكُ الدِّمَاء وَنَحْنُ نُسَبِّحُ بِحَمْدِكَ وَنُقَدِّسُ لَكَ قَالَ إِنِّي أَعْلَمُ مَا لاَ تَعْلَمُونَ {البقرة/30}[183] وَعَلَّمَ آدَمَ الأَسْمَاء كُلَّهَا ثُمَّ عَرَضَهُمْ عَلَى الْمَلَائِكَةِ فَقَالَ أَنبِئُونِي بِأَسْمَاء هَؤُلاء إِن كُنتُمْ صَادِقِينَ {البقرة/31} قَالُواْ سُبْحَانَكَ لاَ عِلْمَ لَنَا إِلاَّ مَا عَلَّمْتَنَا إِنَّكَ أَنتَ الْعَلِيمُ الْحَكِيمُ {البقرة/32}

When we review other beings other than humans and Jinn, one can possibly discuss about absence of pampering of Shaytān on these beings.

In other words, nafs of free-will pampered by Shaytān is possibly only with humans as mentioned[184] أَلَمْ أَعْهَدْ إِلَيْكُمْ يَا بَنِي آدَمَ أَن لاَّ تَعْبُدُوا الشَّيْطَانَ إِنَّهُ لَكُمْ عَدُوٌّ مُّبِينٌ {يس/60}

---

182. My Lord, You have given me [something] of sovereignty and taught me of the interpretation of dreams. Creator of the heavens and earth, You are my protector in this world and in the Hereafter. Cause me to die a Muslim and join me with the righteous."

183. And [mention, O Muhammad], when your Lord said to the angels, "Indeed, I will make upon the earth a successive authority." They said, "Will You place upon it one who causes corruption therein and sheds blood, while we declare Your praise and sanctify You?" Allah said, "Indeed, I know that which you do not know." And He taught Adam the names - all of them. Then He showed them to the angels and said, "Inform Me of the names of these, if you are truthful." They said, "Exalted are You; we have no knowledge except what You have taught us. Indeed, it is You who is the Knowing, the Wise."

184. Did I not enjoin upon you, O children of Adam, that you not worship Satan - [for] indeed, he is to you a clear enemy -

Yet, other beings such as angels and others have knowledge according to their capacity and as bestowed on them by Allah ﷻ and with the permission of Allah ﷻ. This is mentioned as

قَالُواْ سُبْحَانَكَ لاَ عِلْمَ لَنَا إِلاَّ مَا عَلَّمْتَنَا إِنَّكَ أَنتَ الْعَلِيمُ الْحَكِيمُ {البقرة/32}

وَلاَ يُحِيطُونَ بِشَيْءٍ مِّنْ عِلْمِهِ إِلاَّ بِمَا شَاء وَسِعَ كُرْسِيُّهُ السَّمَاوَاتِ وَالأَرْضَ وَلاَ يَؤُودُهُ حِفْظُهُمَا وَهُوَ الْعَلِيُّ الْعَظِيمُ {البقرة/255}[185]

قَالُواْ أَتَجْعَلُ فِيهَا مَن يُفْسِدُ When we review the statement of angels as فِيهَا وَيَسْفِكُ الدِّمَاء وَنَحْنُ نُسَبِّحُ بِحَمْدِكَ وَنُقَدِّسُ لَكَ, this is the angels' statement according to their capacity of knowledge bestowed on them by Allah ﷻ with the permission of Allah ﷻ.

Yet, this is not attitude or expression of arrogance or diseased notions of nafs rendered by free-will or affected by the pampering of Shaytān. No. The statement of angels is just a pure statement for the effort of understanding and possibly puzzlement according to their capacity of I'lm, knowledge and understanding. They mention this reality as[186] قَالُو سُبْحَانَكَ لاَ عِلْمَ لَنَا إِلاَّ مَا عَلَّمْتَنَا إِنَّكَ أَنتَ الْعَلِيمُ الْحَكِيمُ {البقرة/32}.

One should remember that I'lm is the one of the critical essentials after a being is in existence and life as bestowed by Allah ﷻ and permitted by Allah ﷻ.

Yet, this I'lm is given and bestowed by Allah ﷻ at different levels to different beings as mentioned سُبْحَانَكَ and وَلاَ يُحِيطُونَ بِشَيْءٍ مِّنْ عِلْمِهِ إِلاَّ بِمَا شَاء and لاَ عِلْمَ لَنَا إِلاَّ مَا عَلَّمْتَنَا.

Yet, this puzzlement of reality when something may not fully understandable in one's capacity, and effort of understanding can be praiseworthy and essence and purpose of our existence after life is given and bestowed on us by Allah ﷻ. This is mentioned in the episode of Musa as and Khidr in search of I'lm and knowledge. Yet, a lot of cases of puzzlement occurred on the side of Musa as due to his capacity of understanding with his limited given knowledge and ilm bestowed on him by Allah ﷻ.

---

185. , and they encompass not a thing of His knowledge except for what He wills. His Kursi extends over the heavens and the earth, and their preservation tires Him not. And He is the Most High, the Most Great.
186. They said, "Exalted are You; we have no knowledge except what You have taught us. Indeed, it is You who is the Knowing, the Wise."

One can review the ayahs as to realize the puzzlements and thirst for learning on the part of Musa as:[187]

قَالَ لَهُ مُوسَى هَلْ أَتَّبِعُكَ عَلَى أَن تُعَلِّمَنِ مِمَّا عُلِّمْتَ رُشْدًا {الكهف/66}

فَانطَلَقَا حَتَّى إِذَا رَكِبَا فِي السَّفِينَةِ خَرَقَهَا قَالَ أَخَرَقْتَهَا لِتُغْرِقَ أَهْلَهَا لَقَدْ جِئْتَ شَيْئًا إِمْرًا {الكهف/71}[188]

فَانطَلَقَا حَتَّى إِذَا لَقِيَا غُلَامًا فَقَتَلَهُ قَالَ أَقَتَلْتَ نَفْسًا زَكِيَّةً بِغَيْرِ نَفْسٍ لَقَدْ جِئْتَ شَيْئًا نُكُرًا {الكهف/74}[189]

فَانطَلَقَا حَتَّى إِذَا أَتَيَا أَهْلَ قَرْيَةٍ اسْتَطْعَمَا أَهْلَهَا فَأَبَوْا أَن يُضَيِّفُوهُمَا فَوَجَدَا فِيهَا جِدَارًا يُرِيدُ أَنْ يَنقَضَّ فَأَقَامَهُ قَالَ لَوْ شِئْتَ لَاتَّخَذْتَ عَلَيْهِ أَجْرًا {الكهف/77}[190]

Yet, there are certain I'lm that is absolute and real and embodied by all beings as a reality other than some humans and Jinn. This absolute reality and truth is tawhid, Oneness and Uniqueness of Allah ﷻ as Our Creator, Khaliq as[191] هُوَ اللَّهُ أَحَدٌ {الإخلاص/1} اللَّهُ الصَّمَدُ {الإخلاص/2} لَمْ يَلِدْ وَلَمْ يُولَدْ {الإخلاص/3} وَلَمْ يَكُن لَّهُ كُفُوًا أَحَدٌ {الإخلاص/4}.

In these dispositions of certain ilm as an absolute reality and truth, all the beings in the universe take a very uniform determined firm single-minded position against some of these humans and Jinn as[192] تَكَادُ السَّمَاوَاتُ يَتَفَطَّرْنَ مِنْهُ وَتَنشَقُّ الْأَرْضُ وَتَخِرُّ الْجِبَالُ هَدًّا {مريم/90} أَن دَعَوْا لِلرَّحْمَنِ وَلَدًا {مريم/91} وَمَا يَنبَغِي لِلرَّحْمَنِ أَن يَتَّخِذَ وَلَدًا {مريم/92} إِن كُلُّ مَن فِي السَّمَاوَاتِ وَالْأَرْضِ إِلَّا آتِي الرَّحْمَنِ عَبْدًا {مريم/93}.

---

187. Moses said to him, "May I follow you on [the condition] that you teach me from what you have been taught of sound judgement?"

188. So they set out, until when they had embarked on the ship, al-Khidhr tore it open. [Moses] said, "Have you torn it open to drown its people? You have certainly done a grave thing."

189. So they set out, until when they met a boy, al-Khidh r killed him. [Moses] said, "Have you killed a pure soul for other than [having killed] a soul? You have certainly done a deplorable thing."

190. So they set out, until when they came to the people of a town, they asked its people for food, but they refused to offer them hospitality. And they found therein a wall about to collapse, so al-Khidh r restored it. [Moses] said, "If you wished, you could have taken for it a payment."

191. Say, "He is Allah, [who is] One, Allah, the Eternal Refuge. He neither begets nor is born, Nor is there to Him any equivalent."

192. The heavens almost rupture therefrom and the earth splits open and the mountains collapse in devastation That they attribute to the Most Merciful a son. And it is not appropriate for the Most Merciful that He should take a son. There is no one in the heavens and earth but that he comes to the Most Merciful as a servant.

In the case of expanded free will as being the khalîfah of Allah ﷻ on earth, the same offer was made to other beings as mentioned إِنَّا عَرَضْنَا الْأَمَانَةَ عَلَى السَّمَاوَاتِ وَالْأَرْضِ وَالْجِبَالِ فَأَبَيْنَ أَن يَحْمِلْنَهَا وَأَشْفَقْنَ مِنْهَا وَحَمَلَهَا الْإِنسَانُ إِنَّهُ كَانَ ظَلُومًا جَهُولًا {الأحزاب/72}[193]. Yet, by choice these beings did not accept but humans accepted this expanded notion free-will.

One of the examples of differences of attitudes of humans in this notion of free will causing them ظَلُومًا جَهُولًا was possibly their unappreciative behavior compared to constant guidance given by Allah ﷻ by the Qurān and other scriptures as mentioned[194] لَوْ أَنزَلْنَا هَذَا الْقُرْآنَ عَلَى جَبَلٍ لَّرَأَيْتَهُ خَاشِعًا مُّتَصَدِّعًا مِّنْ خَشْيَةِ اللَّهِ وَتِلْكَ الْأَمْثَالُ نَضْرِبُهَا لِلنَّاسِ لَعَلَّهُمْ يَتَفَكَّرُونَ {الحشر/21}.

Yet, the mountains would have a better appreciation with khasyhah of Allah ﷻ to the superior guidance of Allah ﷻ with scriptures and the Qurān. Yet, humans become in different perspectives ظَلُومًا جَهُولًا.

Yet, the case of free will in humans and Jinn have made them immune to fail tests and trials due to arrogance and on the other hand, the case of I'lm and ability to further could have made them differentiate and surpass all other beings due to I'lm and knowledge given and bestowed on them by Allah ﷻ with the permission of Allah ﷻ.

One can consider i'lm as a different type or more I'lm given to humans or Jinn by Allah ﷻ compared to other beings as mentioned[195]

وَعَلَّمَ آدَمَ الْأَسْمَاءَ كُلَّهَا ثُمَّ عَرَضَهُمْ عَلَى الْمَلَائِكَةِ فَقَالَ أَنبِئُونِي بِأَسْمَاءِ هَؤُلَاءِ إِن كُنتُمْ صَادِقِينَ {البقرة/31} قَالُوا سُبْحَانَكَ لَا عِلْمَ لَنَا إِلَّا مَا عَلَّمْتَنَا إِنَّكَ أَنتَ الْعَلِيمُ الْحَكِيمُ {البقرة/32}

---

193. Indeed, we offered the Trust to the heavens and the earth and the mountains, and they declined to bear it and feared it; but man [undertook to] bear it. Indeed, he was unjust and ignorant.
194. If We had sent down this Qur'an upon a mountain, you would have seen it humbled and coming apart from fear of Allah. And these examples We present to the people that perhaps they will give thought.
195. And He taught Adam the names - all of them. Then He showed them to the angels and said, "Inform Me of the names of these, if you are truthful." They said, "Exalted are You; we have no knowledge except what You have taught us. Indeed, it is You who is the Knowing, the Wise."

قَالَ الَّذِي عِندَهُ عِلْمٌ مِّنَ الْكِتَابِ أَنَا آتِيكَ بِهِ قَبْلَ أَن يَرْتَدَّ إِلَيْكَ طَرْفُكَ فَلَمَّا رَآهُ مُسْتَقِرًّا عِندَهُ قَالَ هَذَا مِن فَضْلِ رَبِّي لِيَبْلُوَنِي أَأَشْكُرُ أَمْ أَكْفُرُ وَمَن شَكَرَ فَإِنَّمَا يَشْكُرُ لِنَفْسِهِ وَمَن كَفَرَ فَإِنَّ رَبِّي غَنِيٌّ كَرِيمٌ {النمل/40} [196]

Yet, one can review the below diagram.

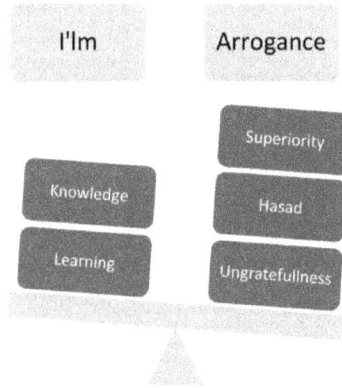

On one side, there is the increased I'lm leading to arrogance and distancing oneself from Allah ﷻ and being lowest of the low of all creation. The example of this Shaytān as mentioned[197] قَالَ يَا إِبْلِيسُ مَا مَنَعَكَ أَن تَسْجُدَ لِمَا خَلَقْتُ بِيَدَيَّ أَسْتَكْبَرْتَ أَمْ كُنتَ مِنَ الْعَالِينَ {ص/75} قَالَ أَنَا خَيْرٌ مِّنْهُ خَلَقْتَنِي مِن نَّارٍ وَخَلَقْتَهُ مِن طِينٍ {ص/76}.

The other is the I'lm that take the person closer to Allah ﷻ and making him possibly surpassing other beings. The role model of this Rasulullah ﷺ as mentioned اقْرَأْ بِاسْمِ رَبِّكَ الَّذِي خَلَقَ {العلق/1} خَلَقَ الْإِنسَانَ مِنْ عَلَقٍ {العلق/2} اقْرَأْ وَرَبُّكَ الْأَكْرَمُ {العلق/3} الَّذِي عَلَّمَ بِالْقَلَمِ {العلق/4} [198] عَلَّمَ الْإِنسَانَ مَا لَمْ يَعْلَمْ {العلق/5}

---

196. Said one who had knowledge from the Scripture, "I will bring it to you before your glance returns to you." And when [Solomon] saw it placed before him, he said, "This is from the favor of my Lord to test me whether I will be grateful or ungrateful. And whoever is grateful - his gratitude is only for [the benefit of] himself. And whoever is ungrateful - then indeed, my Lord is Free of need and Generous."

197. [Allah] said, "O Iblees, what prevented you from prostrating to that which I created with My hands? Were you arrogant [then], or were you [already] among the haughty?" He said, "I am better than him. You created me from fire and created him from clay."

198. Recite in the name of your Lord who created - Created man from a clinging substance. Recite, and your Lord is the most Generous - Who taught by the pen - Taught man that which he knew not.

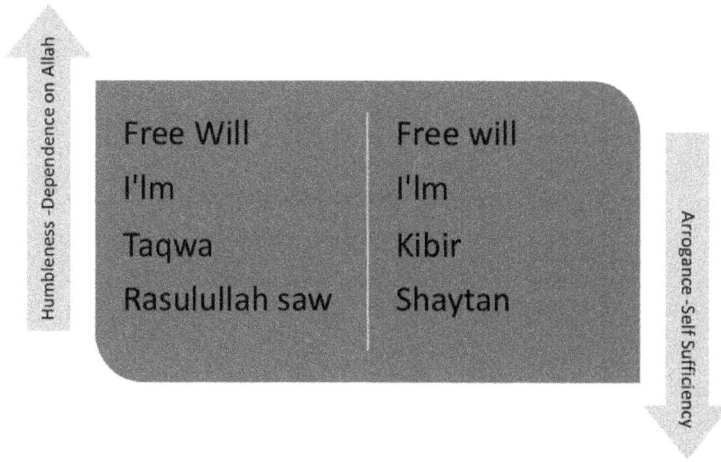

Juz 29

Sûrah 73 al-Muzammil

[1-10]

يَا أَيُّهَا الْمُزَّمِّلُ {المزمل/1} قُمِ اللَّيْلَ إِلَّا قَلِيلًا {المزمل/2} نِصْفَهُ أَوِ انقُصْ مِنْهُ قَلِيلًا {المزمل/3} [199] أَوْ زِدْ عَلَيْهِ وَرَتِّلِ الْقُرْآنَ تَرْتِيلًا {المزمل/4} إِنَّا سَنُلْقِي عَلَيْكَ قَوْلًا ثَقِيلًا {المزمل/5} إِنَّ نَاشِئَةَ اللَّيْلِ هِيَ أَشَدُّ وَطْءًا وَأَقْوَمُ قِيلًا {المزمل/6} إِنَّ لَكَ فِي النَّهَارِ سَبْحًا طَوِيلًا {المزمل/7} وَاذْكُرِ اسْمَ رَبِّكَ وَتَبَتَّلْ إِلَيْهِ تَبْتِيلًا {المزمل/8} رَبُّ الْمَشْرِقِ وَالْمَغْرِبِ لَا إِلَهَ إِلَّا هُوَ فَاتَّخِذْهُ وَكِيلًا {المزمل/9} وَاصْبِرْ عَلَى مَا يَقُولُونَ وَاهْجُرْهُمْ هَجْرًا جَمِيلًا {المزمل/10}

The Reality of the Works of the Dìn

One should realize that a person, who works on the path of Allah ﷻ to please Allah ,ﷻ can slowly increase the responsibility of making dawah to others and take this responsibility overtime as a personal matter.

---

199. O you who wraps himself [in clothing], Arise [to pray] the night, except for a little - Half of it - or subtract from it a little Or add to it, and recite the Qur'an with measured recitation. Indeed, We will cast upon you a heavy word. Indeed, the hours of the night are more effective for concurrence [of heart and tongue] and more suitable for words. Indeed, for you by day is prolonged occupation. And remember the name of your Lord and devote yourself to Him with [complete] devotion. [He is] the Lord of the East and the West; there is no deity except Him, so take Him as Disposer of [your] affairs. And be patient over what they say and avoid t

In other words, the embodiment of ikhlas and working on the path of Allah ﷺ requires personalization of these responsibilities as mentioned[200] لَعَلَّكَ بَاخِعٌ and[201] فَلَعَلَّكَ بَاخِعٌ نَّفْسَكَ عَلَى آثَارِهِمْ إِن لَّمْ يُؤْمِنُوا بِهَذَا الْحَدِيثِ أَسَفًا {الكهف/6} نَّفْسَكَ أَلَّا يَكُونُوا مُؤْمِنِينَ {الشعراء/3}.

These ayahs are not a discouragement or criticism for Rasulullah ﷺ as some of the big belly humans assert on their couches, Astagfirullah. These ayahs are indicating the high maqām of Rasulullah ﷺ as approved and encouraged in his ﷺ personalization of the responsibility of the making dawah or concern of imān for others referred as risālah, or prophethood.

Actually, this is a positive proof that inshAllah, the person does not take the dìn and the matters of the dìn as something of a side occupation and peripheral as today's increasing notions of secularism encourage, but he or she takes all the parts of the dìn as a way of life requiring personalization and embodiment.

This personalization can be in the matters of self-struggle increasing one's I'badah and closeness with Allah ﷺ by implementing different teachings of the Qurān and sunnah of Rasulullah ﷺ in one's life.

On the other hand, this personalization can be in the matters of making dawah to others in relating the dìn. Yet, this part of personalization really truly embodied by Rasulullah ﷺ and all other prophets. Yet, the person always keeps the adab with Allah ﷺ in all types of personalization and remember the traps of Shaytān and the teaching as mentioned[202] إِن وَلَوْ شَاءَ رَبُّكَ and نُّنَزِّلْ عَلَيْهِم مِّنَ السَّمَاءِ آيَةً فَظَلَّتْ أَعْنَاقُهُمْ لَهَا خَاضِعِينَ {الشعراء/4} لَآمَنَ مَن فِي الْأَرْضِ كُلُّهُمْ جَمِيعًا أَفَأَنتَ تُكْرِهُ النَّاسَ حَتَّى يَكُونُوا مُؤْمِنِينَ {يونس/99} وَمَا كَانَ لِنَفْسٍ أَن تُؤْمِنَ إِلَّا بِإِذْنِ اللهِ وَيَجْعَلُ الرِّجْسَ عَلَى الَّذِينَ لَا يَعْقِلُونَ {يونس/100}[203]

Yet, there are the realities of both types of personalization and they are all related.

The true embodiment and personalization of making da'wah requires taking matters personally, worrying about the people, about

200. Then perhaps you would kill yourself through grief over them, [O Muhammad], if they do not believe in this message, [and] out of sorrow.
201. Perhaps, [O Muhammad], you would kill yourself with grief that they will not be believers.
202. If We willed, We could send down to them from the sky a sign for which their necks would remain humbled.
203. And had your Lord willed, those on earth would have believed - all of them entirely. Then, [O Muhammad], would you compel the people in order that they become believers? And it is not for a soul to believe except by permission of Allah, and He will place defilement upon those who will not use reason.

their imān, about their afterlife with also the concern of protecting them from fithnahs and nifāq.

At a closer circle, worrying about the imān of the family members, one's own children, and worrying about the problems of people as a general sensitive responsible person can be some other examples. Allah ﷻ mentions about Rasulullah ﷺ as[204] {107/الأنبياء} وَمَا أَرْسَلْنَاكَ إِلَّا رَحْمَةً لِّلْعَالَمِينَ and[205] {6/الكهف} فَلَعَلَّكَ بَاخِعٌ نَفْسَكَ عَلَى آثَارِهِمْ إِن لَّمْ يُؤْمِنُوا بِهَذَا الْحَدِيثِ أَسَفًا.

Those are all exemplary character of Rasulullah ﷺ for the embodiment of this personalization of this responsibility. Yet, all the teachings of the Qurān and Rasulullah ﷺ tell us how to embody them for our lives.

For a true believer of Allah ﷻ who embodied the teachings of the Qurān and Rasulullah ﷺ, as the true follower of Rasulullah ﷺ, we should also follow our example, al-Habìb ﷺ for the highest maqām of فَلَعَلَّكَ بَاخِعٌ نَفْسَكَ عَلَى آثَارِهِمْ إِن لَّمْ يُؤْمِنُوا بِهَذَا الْحَدِيثِ أَسَفًا {6/الكهف}. This is the utmost concern and worry for the imān of others.

One should remember some of the fuqaha's classification of d'awah or tabligh related with imān as categorized far'z kifāya assumes that Islamic government has the responsibility of this duty of tabligh. Yet, at our times, since, there are no institutions such as Islamic governments, one should remember that the concern and responsibility of imān of others can be currently categorized as far'z a'yn for each individual.

Especially, if a person is living in a non-Muslim dominant society, how can a person truly enjoy their salah, fasting, and all sweet engagements of imān while everyone is spiritually hungry. The neighbor next door, upper and lower are all spiritually hungry with no food of imān.

Spiritual hunger can lead to worse deaths than physical hunger. Both types of hunger should be addressed and the people who have some physical and spiritual food of imān as the sunnah of Rasulullah ﷺ should share.

Yes, this agitated state of[206] فَلَعَلَّكَ بَاخِعٌ نَفْسَكَ عَلَى آثَارِهِمْ إِن لَّمْ يُؤْمِنُوا بِهَذَا الْحَدِيثِ أَسَفًا {6/الكهف} can be supported and transformed into a higher maqam

---

204. And We have not sent you, [O Muhammad], except as a mercy to the worlds.
205. Then perhaps you would kill yourself through grief over them, [O Muhammad], if they do not believe in this message, [and] out of sorrow.
206. Then perhaps you would kill yourself through grief over them, [O Muhammad], if they do not believe in this message, [and] out of sorrow.

with night prayers, tahajjud and night engagements of solo and private relationship with Allah ﷻ in crying, discharging and getting empowered against these agitating, shocking and terrifying states of responsibility of sharing and helping people. These night engagements with Allah ﷻ through worship and personal connection through tahajjud and ibadah and recitation of the Qurān can transform the person to maqāmu-mahmūd as mentioned[207] وَمِنَ اللَّيْلِ فَتَهَجَّدْ بِهِ نَافِلَةً لَّكَ عَسَى أَن يَبْعَثَكَ رَبُّكَ مَقَامًا مَّحْمُودًا {الإسراء/79}.

If we want to be the true followers of the Leader of maqāmu-mahmūd, al-Habib, Rasulullah ﷺ, then we should also have the reflections of this maqām with our tahajjud and night prayers and recitation of the Qurān.

Yes, it can be difficult to wake up for tahajjud with all the pranks of Shaytān and the nafs, yet, the person should do their utmost effort to get up and jump up like a rocket as a possible indications of suggested action with the beginning of the two Sūrahs with the same word as قُم mentioned as[208] {المزمل/2} قُمِ اللَّيْلَ إِلاَّ قَلِيلاً and[209] {المدثر/2} قُمْ فَأَنذِرْ. Yes, the word قُم can indicate throwing oneself from the bed like a rocket to cracks and unshatter the pranks of Shaytān and nafs in order to be in the high positive states of sakina, energy and power from Allah ﷻ in tahajjud and night prayers through the recitation of the Qurān and talking to Allah ﷻ and explaining all one's problems to Allah ﷻ with crying, and asking help and solutions. Although Allah ﷻ is aware of everything internal and external engagements of the person, dua is the essence of 'ibadah when the person expresses this need in front of Rabbul Alamin as the a'bd of Allah ﷻ.

One should remember that when a person is worried about anything either related with dunya-world with lowly worries or about the imān of others, they can both put the person in the agitated, and depressive states of self-destruction of pessimism.

The people getting nightmares at night and not properly sleeping can be some outcomes of both of these agitated states of worry, terror and spiritual panic.

Yet, the person who is agitated about the worries of others for their imān can receive high maqams and rewards from Allah ﷻ. On the other

---

207. And from [part of] the night, pray with it as additional [worship] for you; it is expected that your Lord will resurrect you to a praised station.
208. Arise [to pray] the night, except for a little -
209. Arise and warn

hand, the person who puts him or herself in the agitated states due to lowly issues of world can ruin both their life here and afterlife.

Yet, the person who is agitated due to worries of imān for others, Allah ﷻ shows a way of exit to remove these states and transform them into endurable states by reliance on Allah ﷻ with night prayers, tahajjud and recitation of the Qurān at night as mentioned[210] {المزمل/9} فَاتَّخِذْهُ وَكِيلاً.

In this Sûrah, Allah ﷻ underlines these exit points with the tahajjud prayers, recitation of the Qurān and 'ibadah as mentioned[211] يَا أَيُّهَا الْمُزَّمِّلُ {المزمل/1} قُمِ اللَّيْلَ إِلَّا قَلِيلاً {المزمل/2} نِصْفَهُ أَوِ انقُصْ مِنْهُ قَلِيلًا {المزمل/3} أَوْ زِدْ عَلَيْهِ وَرَتِّلِ الْقُرْآنَ تَرْتِيلًا {المزمل/4}.

The noble responsibility of risalah and the responsibility of imān of people as a difficult task of freezing the human faculties with due to its complications can be indicated in[212] إِنَّا سَنُلْقِي عَلَيْكَ قَوْلاً ثَقِيلاً {المزمل/5} and[213] إِنَّ لَكَ فِي النَّهَارِ سَبْحًا طَوِيلًا {المزمل/7}.

The necessity of discharge at night to Allah ﷻ as mentioned[214] إِنَّ نَاشِئَةَ اللَّيْلِ هِيَ أَشَدُّ وَطْءًا وَأَقْوَمُ قِيلًا {المزمل/6} in order to focus only as the One Who is the True Source of Allah Power and Help can be indicated as[215] وَاذْكُرِ اسْمَ رَبِّكَ وَتَبَتَّلْ إِلَيْهِ تَبْتِيلًا {المزمل/8} رَبُّ الْمَشْرِقِ وَالْمَغْرِبِ لَا إِلَهَ إِلَّا هُوَ فَاتَّخِذْهُ وَكِيلًا {المزمل/9}.

One should remember that the embodiment of sabr-patience and having still pleasant mubasarrahat-interaction with humans, and handling the related problems are not easy. Yet, both the implementation of sabr and pleasant, kind and gentle interaction with humans can be achieved through night engagements of prayers and recitation of the Qurān and tahajjud.

Allahumma Ja'alna min al-Mutahajjidin bi-Fadlika, bi hurmati Habibuka man yakanu lahu maqāmu mahmûd, ﷺ, Amìn.

---

210. [He is] the Lord of the East and the West; there is no deity except Him, so take Him as Disposer of [your] affairs.

211. O you who wraps himself [in clothing], Arise [to pray] the night, except for a little - Half of it - or subtract from it a little Or add to it, and recite the Qur'an with measured recitation.

212. Indeed, We will cast upon you a heavy word.

213. Indeed, for you by day is prolonged occupation.

214. Indeed, the hours of the night are more effective for concurrence [of heart and tongue] and more suitable for words.

215. And remember the name of your Lord and devote yourself to Him with [complete] devotion. [He is] the Lord of the East and the West; there is no deity except Him, so take Him as Disposer of [your] affairs.

BIBLIOGRAPHY

[1] U. P. Oxford, «Oxford Dictionaries,» 2016. [Online]. Available: http://www.oxforddictionaries.com/us/definition/american_ english/. [Accessed 2016].

[2] S. Abu-Dawud, Sunan Abu Dawud, Riyadh: Darussalam, 2008.

[3] M. Al-Bukhari, The translation of the meanings of Sahih Al-Bukhari, Kazi Publications, 1986.

[4] A. Muslim, Sahih Muslim (translated by Siddiqui, A.), Peace Vision, 1972.

[5] M. Tirmizi, Jami At-Tirmizi, Dar-us-Salam, 2007.

AUTHOR BIO

Dr. Kumek had classical training in Islamic sciences from the respected Shuyûqh/Teachers of Turkey, India, Egypt, Yemen, Somalia, Morocco, Sudan, and the United States. He stayed and studied classical Islamic sciences in Egypt and Turkey as well.

In his Western training, education and teaching experience, Dr. Kumek has acted as the religious studies coordinator at State University of New York (SUNY) Buffalo State and taught undergraduate and graduate courses in religious studies at SUNY at Buffalo State, Niagara University, Daemen College and Harvard Divinity School. Dr. Kumek also pursued doctorate degree in physics at SUNY at Buffalo published academic papers in the areas of quantum physics and medical physics. Then, he decided to engage with the world of social sciences through social anthropology, education, and cultural anthropology in his doctorate studies and subsequently, spent a few years as a research associate in the anthropology department of the same university and subsequently, completed a postdoctoral fellowship at Harvard Divinity school. Some of his book titles include sociology through religion, religious literacy through ethnography, selected passages from the Qurãn, selected passages from the Hadith (titled as Rasulullah ﷺ) and selected prayers of the Prophet Muhammad ﷺ (titled as Pearls and Diamonds). Dr. M. Yunus Kumek is currently teaching on Muslim Ministry and Spiritual Care at Harvard Divinity School.

ACKNOWLEDGMENTS

I would like to thank all my unnamed teachers, friends, and students for their input, ideas, suggestions, help, and support during and before the preparation of this book.

I would like to thank Dr. David Banks, faculty of the Department of Anthropology, State University of New York (SUNY), Sister Toni Hajdaj, Sister Umm Aisha, Dr. AbdulAhad, Br. Ali Rifat and His wife Sister Yildiz at-Turki, Sheikh Dr. Omar of Maryland al-Hindi, Sheikh Tamer of Buffalo, and Sheikh Ali of Hartford Seminary, Sisters Asya Hamad, Amina Osman, and Fatima Samrodia of Darul-Ulum Madania of Buffalo for all their editing, suggestions and comments.

I want to also thank the team of Medina House Publishing in all their preparations and efforts at all stages of this book especially Br. Murat, Br. Khalid (Halit), Br. Mehmet (Matt) and Sister Karen.

Lastly, I would like to thank all of my family members for their patience with me during the preparation of this book.

We ask Allah ﷻ to accept all our efforts with the Divine Karam, Fadl, and Grace but not with our faulty and limited efforts deeming rejection.
اللَّهُمَّ صلِّ عَلى سَيِّدِناَ وَ حَبِيْبَنَا وَ مَوْلَانَا مُحَمَّد.

Index

www.ingramcontent.com/pod-product-compliance
Lightning Source LLC
Chambersburg PA
CBHW032055090426
42744CB00005B/232